"Eighty-five percent of American Christians describe themselves as 'defeated by temptation and life-controlling problems.' That's insane, yet that's exactly what Arnie Cole and Michael Ross discovered in Back to the Bible's latest research. And that's why they wrote *Tempted, Tested, True*. It's a must-read for churches, families—everyone!"

—Susie Shellenberger, editor of *Sisterhood* magazine and the author of 51 books, including *What Your Daughter Isn't Telling You*

Arnie Cole (EdD, Pepperdine) is the CEO of Back to the Bible and director of research and development for the Center for Bible Engagement. He and his wife, Char, live near Lincoln, Nebraska. Learn more at www.backtothebible.org.

Michael Ross is an award-winning journalist. He writes, edits, and manages Back to the Bible's book publishing effort and is a former editor of *Breakaway* magazine. He has authored or collaborated on more than 30 books, including *What Your Son Isn't Telling You*. The Ross family lives in Lincoln, Nebraska.

Tempted, Tested, True

A Proven Path to Overcoming
Soul-Robbing Choices

Arnie Cole and Michael Ross

BETHANY HOUSE PUBLISHERS

a division of Baker Publishing Group
Minneapolis, Minnesota

© 2013 by Arnie Cole and Michael Ross

Published by Bethany House Publishers
11400 Hampshire Avenue South
Bloomington, Minnesota 55438
www.bethanyhouse.com

Bethany House Publishers is a division of
Baker Publishing Group, Grand Rapids, Michigan

Printed in the United States of America

Library of Congress Cataloging-in-Publication Data
Cole, Arnie.
    Tempted, tested, true : a proven path to overcoming soul-robbing choices / Arnie Cole and Michael Ross.
      p. cm.
    Summary: "Ministry leader uses survey research and personal narratives to teach readers the most effective ways to overcome temptation"—Provided by publisher.
    Includes bibliographical references.
    ISBN 978-0-7642-1085-3 (pbk. : alk. paper)
    1. Temptation. 2. Success—Religious aspects—Christianity. I. Ross, Michael, 1961– II. Title.
BT725.C65 2013
241'.3—dc23   2012040438

In keeping with biblical principles of creation stewardship, Baker Publishing Group advocates the responsible use of our natural resources. As a member of the Green Press Initiative, our company uses recycled paper when possible. The text paper of this book is composed in part of post-consumer waste.

Cover design by Lookout Design, Inc.

The authors are represented by WordServe Literary Group

13 14 15 16 17 18 19   7 6 5 4 3 2 1

Dedication

From Arnie

For two great guys—Bill Bantz and Harold Berry. Thanks, Bill, for encouraging me to pursue the dream of evangelism by daily spiritual growth. And thanks, Harold, for teaching me the power of praying with a friend. You've both reminded me that, regardless of age, temptation leaves no one untouched.

And for one incredible woman—my wife, Char. After twenty years, you still cry when I leave for faraway places. You're amazing!

From Michael

For Pastor Brad and Rhonda Carpenter . . . and my whole Connecting Pointe family.

For Tiffany and Christopher. I love you more and more each day.

For Jerry. Your name doesn't flash on my phone screen these days, but your influence will always be with me. I miss you.

"Keep your eyes on *Jesus*, who both began and finished this race we're in. Study how he did it. Because he never lost sight of where he was headed—that exhilarating finish in and with God—he could put up with anything along the way: Cross, shame, whatever. And now he's *there*, in the place of honor, right alongside God. When you find yourselves flagging in your faith, go over that story again, item by item, that long litany of hostility he plowed through. *That* will shoot adrenaline into your souls!" (Hebrews 12:2–3 THE MESSAGE).

Acknowledgments

So many people helped us shape this book, as well as our previous one, *Unstuck: Your Life. God's Design. Real Change.* We'd like to especially thank these friends:

Tami Weissert—executive vice president of Back to the Bible. Her blogs and her radio and speaking platforms have helped us get noticed in this noisy world.

Dr. Pamela Ovwigho—executive director of the Center for Bible Engagement. She has spent the past seven years analyzing the spiritual lives of more than 100,000 people, and then she shared her findings with us. (See chapters 4 and 5.)

Jack Burke—assistant to the CEO. He crisscrosses the nation, generating excitement for our Bible engagement message, as well as our mobile spiritual-growth tool. (Check out *goTandem.com.*)

Tiffany Ross—wife, mother, and children's director at Connecting Pointe Church in Lincoln, Nebraska. Her theological insights and commonsense ministry instincts have been woven into these pages.

Char Cole—wife, mother, co-owner of Still Waters Ranch in Hickman, Nebraska. She read every word within these pages, and then gave her thumbs-up *before* we went to press. Her editorial suggestions helped us craft a powerful resource.

Greg Johnson—president of WordServe Literary Group in Colorado. He's much, much more than an agent. He's our brother in Christ!

Three talented colleagues at Back to the Bible/go *Tandem* who are assisting us with design, sales, and marketing—Meredith Megrue, Rhonda Carpenter, and Kevin Sheen.

Top-notch freelance writers who shared their stories with us— Theresa Cox (chapter 2), David Barshinger, PhD (chapter 3), Kelly Combs (chapter 6), Sue Cameron (chapter 8), Deidra Riggs (chapters 9 and 10), Michelle DeRusha ("Ending Point").

The Minnesota-based editorial and marketing teams at Bethany House—Christopher Soderstrom, Julie Smith, Andy McGuire, Brett Benson, Carra Carr, Tim Peterson, Steve Oates, David Horton, and Jim Parrish.

Contents

Starting Point

Immobilized and Neutralized

"This is goodbye," said Jesus. . . . "I'm going home. My Father in heaven is waiting for me."
"Don't go just yet," said James. "Stay awhile."
"We can get something to eat, build a fire, have good talks," said Nathaniel Bartholomew.
"Like old times," said Peter.
"No more old times," said Jesus. "There are only new times from now on. . . ."[1]

Impossible! I think as I cling to a steep rock face. *How'd I ever get talked into this? I'd rather be sitting in a warm cabin . . . even just by a warm campfire—where it's safe. NOT risking life and limb on a fifty-foot cliff. This is absolutely INSANE.*

I (Michael) am on a ten-day backpacking trip in California's Ansel Adams Wilderness with a bunch of guy friends. We're undergoing a "build confidence and conquer your fear" quest of sorts. Today's challenge: Scale a slick canyon wall.

I slide my right hand across a boulder and feel a tiny crevice. I grip it with my fingertips and push with my legs.

As I inch my way up—and begin to trust the safety harness around my waist—it isn't long before I discover that this climb isn't all that crazy after all. The only truly scary part is wearing a blindfold. That's right, a bandanna covers my eyes. I can't see a thing!

"Excellent, Mike—you're doing great!" yells a voice from below. It's my friend Tom. He's my climbing partner and, literally, my eyes during this exercise.

"Listen to my voice," he calls. "I'll get you to the top. Trust me." I stretch to reach and dig my fingers into another crevice.

"That's it!" Tom shouts. "Now push with your legs again. Only another three feet and you're there!"

I'm way out of my comfort zone. In fact, I've been living on the edge all week, pushing my body and facing challenge after challenge. The point is to take what I learn in the wilderness and apply it to my life back home—especially to my faith. I have to admit it: I've gotten way too comfortable . . . preferring my old ways, frequently if not constantly going with what I know, regularly resisting anything new. And when it comes to struggles and temptations, too often I'm finding myself immobilized and neutralized.

Now suddenly, confusion. I can't hear Tom's voice. Some of the other guys are attempting to guide me, each in a different way.

"Go to the left!" someone yells.

"No—move to your right."

"Push harder!"

Tom comes to the rescue: *"Quiet."* After a few moments of silence, I hear his voice again. "Listen to me. Reach for a handhold above your head, push with your legs, and you'll be at the top."

His instructions are perfect. And before I can think about it again, I've reached my destination. *Victory!* I hear applause from other members of my group.

I pull off the bandanna, feeling confident, and look down. *Should have stuck with the blindfold!*

🍎   🍎   🍎

Back at home within the safety of the four walls of our family room, I sit by a fire, nibble on a snack, and relive my recent mountaintop experiences. While I prefer the comforts and routine of daily living, it occurs to me that I rarely have felt more alive than when I found myself dangling from a rock face. God definitely had my attention, and my trust.

Am I too distracted, Lord? I pray. *Is that why I struggle so? Am I not really hearing you?*

Opening a book, I begin to read.

This One who walks like a king is named Jesus. They called Him the Nazarene or the Galilean. He called Himself the Son of man.

The common people speak of Him softly, with deep affection, such as the shepherds know, who carry their little lambs in their bosoms.

The beggars whisper His name in the streets as they pass, and the children may be heard singing about Him. His name has been breathed in prayer and whispered at night under the stars. He is known to the diseased, the human flotsam and jetsam that shuffles in and out of the towns and drifts hopelessly along the dusty highways of human misery.

His fame has trickled down to the streets of forgotten men, has seeped into the shadowed refuges of the unremembered women. It is Jesus of Nazareth.

Any outcast could tell you of Him. There are women whose lives have been changed who could tell you of Him—but not without tears. There are silent men—walking strangely as if unaccustomed to it—who speak of Him with lights in their eyes.

It is Jesus whom they are crowding to see. They want to look on His face to see the quality of His expression that seems to promise so much to the weary and heavy-laden; that look that seems to offer healing of mind and soul and body; forgiveness of sin; another chance—a beginning again.

His look seemed to sing of tomorrow—a new tomorrow—in which there should be no more pain, no more suffering, nor persecution, nor cruelty, nor hunger, nor neglect, nor disillusionments, nor broken promises, nor death.[2]

🍎 🍎 🍎

Lord, I've lived like a prodigal without even realizing it. I want that light in my eyes again. I want the new, but I'm not sure how to find it.

As I pray and read and ponder, Scripture reveals some answers. . . .

God is always at work . . . creating, perfecting, regenerating—reclaiming what is His. He knows exactly what I need and how to work out the new and destroy the old. A believer walks with the protection of our Lord Jesus Christ. Even though He calls me to bear some burdens, some hurts, and some trials, He will continue to work in me, giving me a heart like His. This is my highest calling: living in respectful fear of the One who spoke the universe into being and who holds me in the palm of His loving hand.

Disobedience can result in devastating consequences. I read about King David's life. Even though he was completely forgiven for his acts of lust, adultery, theft, and murder, God did not remove the consequences of his sin. *What can I learn from this?* Maybe that He wants me to have a serious reverence for His instructions. And that when I blow it, He wants me to take responsibility for my actions by turning to Him in repentance. He will drive out the fear of doubt and condemnation and give me the courage to follow His lead as I deal with the consequences.

He stepped down to save me and to bear the punishment for all my sins. He bought my freedom and gives back complete forgiveness. This all-powerful God is tender toward me and will never give me more than I can bear. He will always watch over me with a steady eye. He never blinks. I *can* trust Him.

When Prodigals Come Home

When he was still a long way off, his father saw him. His heart pounding, he ran out, embraced him, and kissed him. The son started his speech: "Father, I've sinned against God, I've sinned before you; I don't deserve to be called your son ever again."

But the father wasn't listening. He was calling to the servants, "Quick. Bring a clean set of clothes and dress him. Put the family ring on his finger and sandals on his feet. Then get a grain-fed heifer and roast it. We're going to feast! We're going to have a wonderful time! My son is here—given up for dead and now alive! Given up for lost and now found!" And they began to have a wonderful time.[3]

Michael is a prodigal. *Each of us is.*

God's ways are simply not our ways. Our hearts are restless and tend to wander; our selfish wills and ill-advised choices end up usurping His place, leaving us feeling lost, miserable, and defeated.

Some of us have tiptoed back to Him in fear and trembling, expecting a firm smack and a wagging finger. We've expected, and deserved, the "I told you you'd mess it up" speeches and the "Where in the world have you been?" questions.[4] But Jesus throws His arms around us, assures us that no matter where we go, He'll never lose us, reminds us of the eternal home He's given us with Him. He washes us clean. And then He throws a party on our behalf.

All Jesus asks in return is one thing: *Believe in Him.*

🍎   🍎   🍎

By this point in our lives, we've figured out that the path home isn't easy. (It never has been, never will be.) And believing is sometimes hard too. The steps we must take so God can demolish the old and fashion the new often feel terrifying. As He goes about His work, we sometimes feel alone; often we feel judged by those inside *and* outside the church.

And all along the way, temptation nips at our heels. It never lets up.

Temptation frequently finds a way to deceive us and knock us off course. Before we know it, our faith has stopped moving. We end up paralyzed—literally immobilized, and neutralized by sin. Just look around. Everyone struggles with something. Mark feels trapped by lust. Alyssa gossips. Blaine overeats. Mary's arrogant. Kelly's mom drinks heavily. Randy has mistaken a greedy vice for a noble virtue. They're all believers.

Yet for Christians, the truth is that meaningful change and real transformation are within reach. So why aren't our lives different? Why don't we experience less anxiety, less despair, less rage? Why don't we experience more joy, more freedom, more fulfillment?

Current research by the Center for Bible Engagement indicates that more than 85 percent of American Christians describe themselves as "defeated by temptation and life-controlling problems"—everything from sexual addiction and pornography to lying, cheating, stealing, gossiping, lustfulness, greed, and jealousy. As a result, many have fallen into a toxic downward spiral:

(1) They struggle alone.
(2) They neglect the very things that can help them break free—
     prayer, Bible engagement, and true community.
(3) They give up spiritually.

They forget this reality: God isn't at all shocked by our weaknesses. God doesn't stop loving us when we fail. God never gives up on any of us, not for a moment. His heart breaks when sin causes us to run *from* Him instead of *to* Him.

C. S. Lewis said it so well: "Only those who try to resist temptation know how strong it is."[5] And no one understands temptation's
power better than Jesus. On earth, He faced the same enticements
we encounter yet never once yielded to them. And as God, he broke
the grip of the horrors our sin causes. *Only* Jesus fully knows what temptation is and how we can
overcome it. We *can* realize lasting change, through Him. He invites
us to a better life—the very best life—and He extends His loving
hand to guide us toward it.

Why Do We Shrink Away From Christ's Healing Touch?

Our interviews with experts and ordinary folks alike have yielded
some clues.

We Excuse Our Behavior

Temptation rarely marches into our lives with announcements
of its hostile intentions. Instead, it perverts reality and cloaks itself
as an excusable action, even as a commendable trait. W. Jay Wood,
professor of philosophy at Wheaton College, observes:

> Inordinate anger masquerades as "righteous indignation," arrogance
> as "standing up for my rights," lust as "healthy romantic ardor." When
> it comes to temptation and sin, we're all inveterate spin doctors.[6]

We Ignore the "S" Word

Saying the word *sin* in public is like saying *bomb* on a plane.
It's a loaded word that makes us uncomfortable. One person's
perception of sin may be different from another's. And we don't
want to sound harsh or judgmental, so we avoid using the term.
That's a problem. Scot McKnight explains:

A whole generation has been nurtured on a message that has embraced a gracious view of God, but has far too often ignored the zealous holiness of that same God's love. We're in a dangerous place today. We need to confront again the message of the Bible about sin.[7]

We Misuse God's Grace

A growing number of us have become apathetic about sin, disinterested in holiness. Amy, for instance, says, "I'm not denying that I fall short, [but] I just don't see the point in dwelling on it. God forgives, and I'm free in Him." It's almost like saying, "Grace allows me to live however I please."

That bird doesn't fly. Jesus didn't sacrifice himself and defeat death so we could go on just as we are; He did it because otherwise we *would* have continued as before, and because in that state we'd have been separated from Him forever. The question isn't whether God still loves us when we sin—it's why we'd want to go on in slavery when God laid down His own life so we could be free. To paraphrase Leighton Ford, God loves us exactly as we are, and He loves us far too much to want us to stay that way.

Nobody conquers sin on their own. Through the power of God's Spirit, though, we can be freed from its grip. Because of Jesus, we *can* change soul-robbing behaviors and find relief from the entanglements and traps that so many times, for so long, have snared us and pulled us down.

It all begins when we face a truth we've tried to avoid and ignore: *Everyone* struggles with temptation, and *every* sin is deadly. There's no offense that doesn't erode us from the inside out—damaging our integrity, obscuring our identity, and weakening our relationships.

All sin impedes our intimacy with God and inhibits our ability to truly love one another.

God makes clear the solution: We have certain hope through faith.[8]

David gave us a foretaste of this truth:

> Blessed is the one whose transgression is forgiven,
> whose sin is covered.
> Blessed is the man against whom the LORD counts
> no iniquity,
> and in whose spirit there is no deceit.[9]

When we turn to Jesus and rely on Him, He deals with our struggles—moment by moment, hour by hour, day by day. He also works from the inside out, counteracting the poisonous effects of sin—healing what is hurt, restoring what is lost, strengthening what is weak.

What You'll Find in *Tempted, Tested, True*

I'm Arnie Cole, CEO of Back to the Bible. My writing partner is Michael Ross, an award-winning journalist and author of thirty-two books. Together, we've seen real and lasting change during our fifty-plus years of combined ministry experience. And as a behaviorist, I've charted successful spiritual growth programs for fellow "wounded strugglers."

My nationwide research with more than 100,000 Christians has formed the empirical foundation for this book. We'll show you proven ways to neutralize temptation—to evade its grip and to unplug its power so as to steer clear of its disastrous consequences.

Here's what we've packed into this unique resource:

Two Books in One

(1) A faith-building guide filled with practical solutions
(2) A personal and small-group workbook

Explore these pages on your own, referring back to them as often as you would with any practical reference guide. Better yet, read it with friends in any type of small group. All chapters can benefit both men and women. Also included is a Web-based link you can use for both personal application and group Bible study.

Real-Life Stories That Chart Lasting Change

You'll be inspired by moving testimonies:

Kelly—opens up about the struggles of caring for an alcoholic parent.

Michael—guides you through the stumbling blocks of worry and fear.

Mark—talks candidly about his addiction to pornography.

Danielle—unlocks truths about real love.

Cheryl—reveals the difference transparent community makes.

Michelle—encourages each of us to learn what God really thinks of us.

In our situation, writing together, using the personal pronoun *I* can get a little confusing, so to keep things simple, we'll indicate who is speaking. (For example, in chapter 1 it's Arnie; in chapter 2 it's Mike. In some chapters it's another contributing storyteller.) The collective *we* refers to both of us and you . . . strugglers who want to live more like Jesus every day.

A Gentle "Nudge"

In the words of one Christ-follower we interviewed: "Mix Scripture with the encouragement of believers who gently nudge but don't judge, and you've got a powerful way of breaking free from Satan's attacks."

So think of this section in each chapter as a nudge from us. The nudges aren't based only on our opinions but are drawn from detailed, quantifiable research and interviews conducted with fellow strugglers (experts and ordinary folks alike).

This is also the book's roll-up-your-sleeves-and-dive-into-Scripture aspect, and the idea is this: *God's Word, hidden in my heart, fortifies me against temptation's power.*[10]

The nudges you'll find:

Nudge One: Learn to Be God-Centered

Nudge Two: Pinpoint Your Weaknesses

Nudge Three: Reconsider Holiness

Nudge Four: Change Your Brain

Nudge Five: Interrupt Your Heart

Nudge Six: "Detach" Attachments

Nudge Seven: Surrender Control

Nudge Eight: Shake the Shame

Nudge Nine: Fall in Love Again

Nudge Ten: Rethink Church

Here's how each entry is divided:

TEMPTED—*Identifying Soul-Robbing Traps*

First, we look inward and evaluate our struggles. Admitting our temptations and bringing them before God is the first step toward overcoming them and charting a path toward growth.

TESTED—*Learning How to Break Free*

Next, we highlight what works for other believers. Our conclusions about why we struggle, and what helps us to break free, are drawn from years of research.[11]

TRUE—*Charting a Path Toward Lasting Change*

Finally, we help you customize a realistic "change plan" you can apply to your life. Grounded in God's Word, it will challenge you to engage, reflect on, and live it out practically, day by day.

A Nationwide Research Study

My team and I (Arnie) at the Center for Bible Engagement began studying the spiritual lives of Christ-followers to answer a deceptively simple question: *Why do so many of us own Bibles yet so few of us read them?* It soon became clear that the lack of Bible engagement was *not* because we don't see God's Word as important, or don't believe it, or don't understand it. Rather, people say time and again that they want to hear from God through His Word but are simply "too busy." This, in turn, led us to consider how temptation could be holding people back from growing spiritually.

In 2008, we launched our first major study of temptation. We discussed many findings from that initial study in our first book, *Unstuck*. Since that time, we've completed surveys on temptation and spiritual growth with more than 100,000 people. Our participants are a diverse group in every sense of the word—ranging in age from thirteen to over seventy, representing every state in the U.S., in addition to twenty other countries.

Through these surveys, we've learned that . . .

- the temptation to do or have something you know you shouldn't is universal among humans.
- on an average day, most people encounter three to five temptations.
- men typically experience more temptations than women.
- temptations change over time. When we're young, physically oriented temptations have the most pull; later in life, struggles with pride and judging others become more prominent.

The world breaks everyone, and afterward,
many are strong at the broken places.

—ERNEST HEMINGWAY

An Opportunity to Engage the Bible

Once again, we can be radically better (truly strengthened and renewed) if we allow God to speak to us through His Word. *Bible engagement* is the key. And as we seek to live out these words that are taking root and then blooming vitally in us, God shows us how to impact the world for Him—helping others, loving the unlovely, reaching out to the needy.

Bible engagement boils down to three simple facets:

(1) Stop simply *reading* the Bible, and start *engaging* it. It's essential that we consistently *receive*, *reflect on*, and *respond to* God's Word.

(2) Pay close attention to frequency. We've found, repeatedly: Engaging Scripture four or more times per week makes the biggest difference.

(3) Consider what the Bible is: our personal connection with God. It's how we hear from and have a two-way conversation with our Creator.

In order to grow, a relationship needs consistent connection. We draw closer to our loved ones as we spend time with them. It's the same way with Christ. Engaging the Bible and hearing the Lord's voice through Scripture must be experienced personally and regularly.

The Bible has a supernatural component no one can explain. For me, the more I engage the Scriptures—and respond to what God says—the more my life is molded into what He designed me to be. And even though I can learn a lot through Bible reading, there's something on a relational plane that's even more exciting and more transformational. God's Word gets past my head, touches my heart, and revives my soul. Most of all, it renews my mind and begins to reproduce God's nature and character in my life.

(You can learn more about Bible engagement in our first book: *Unstuck: Your Life. God's Design. Real Change.* See www.unstuck. goTandem.com.)

Tempted, Tested, True Is Online

We also introduce *goTandem*—a website that can help you and your church grow. Pop over anytime for video clips, spiritual growth assessments, and additional faith-building resources (**www.temptedbook.com**).

1

From the Garden to the Desert . . . and On to the Cross

Our Age-Old Battle With a Deadly Menace

"Religion is for people who are afraid they'll go to hell. Spirituality is for people who have been there."[1]

God speaks. Darkness hides. A soup of nothingness suddenly bursts with light and color and warmth.

God creates—water, air, sky, earth. And living beings!

Creatures spring forth in every size and shape, splashing through the seas and thundering across the plains. Chirping. Flapping. Swarming. Bleating. Gnawing. Clawing. Digging.

It is good.[2]

God gives. His essence. His heart. Himself.

As He reaches into the ground, dust pours through His fingers. But then He begins to form it, molding sand and mud into something familiar. A foot. An arm. A face. His greatest masterpiece.

> Let us make human beings in our image,
> make them reflecting our nature
> So they can be responsible
> for the fish in the sea, the birds in the air, the cattle,
> And, yes, Earth itself,
> and every animal that moves on the face of Earth.[3]

God animates. Lungs inflate. Hearts beat. Eyes open wide—gazing back into His.

Humans: spirit, flesh, reason, emotion, passion, creativity, intellect. The finest reflection of God that He could dream up. His image. His family. Adam and Eve.

God blesses. And the first man and woman rule over the world.

> Prosper! Reproduce! Fill Earth! Take charge!
> Be responsible for fish in the sea and birds in the air,
> for every living thing that moves on the face of Earth.[4]

God rests. The world is complete. His work is finished.

> It is good, so very good.[5]

🍎 🍎 🍎

In the beginning, life was flawless.

Adam and Eve lived in a garden paradise "to work it and take care of it."[6] It was their vocation, their life's purpose. God spoke intimately with His children there and even walked among them "in the cool of the day."[7]

Imagine it: Two perfect humans enjoying pristine perfection with their Maker. No fear or shame came between them and God. No pain, no suffering, no hatred, no regrets. Perfect harmony. Adam was one note, Eve the other, and God the third—woven together in an intimate melody none of us has ever come close to recapturing.[8] Way different from today, right?

I (Arnie) see brokenness all around me. In my own town—a relatively affluent Nebraska community—children and homeless families go hungry. Some huddle near busy intersections, clutching tattered signs: "Need Food." "Unemployed Vet." "Help My Kids." Teens who look like streetwalkers and gang-bangers file into our schools.

I flip on the news and am assaulted by a barrage of nonstop misery: rising gas prices, crashing markets; earthquakes along the Pacific Rim, tornadoes in the Midwest. "Terrorists mastermind another bombing . . ." "Scandal on Capitol Hill . . ." "A deadly shooting *inside* a mega-church . . ."

Man's inhumanity to man. Fractured families. Broken hearts. Lying. Cheating. Stealing. Rage. Envy. Gossip. Greed. Pride. *Sin.*

Everywhere. All around us and *in* us—you, me . . . our children. No one is immune. Yet on most days we manage to stay pretty numb to it all. "We ignore our failures and downplay our moral meltdowns," writes Steven James. "We fill our lives with frantic distractions so we can avoid noticing the splinter of guilt embedded so deeply in our souls."[9]

The question is, why do we have a splinter in our souls?

Genesis 3 tells us *what* happened in the garden: *The serpent shows up, a lie about God is whispered, a soul-robbing choice is made, forbidden fruit is tasted, and . . . BAM! Humans are tossed into the thorns of a fallen world.*

Adam and Eve were made in the image of God. An image represents someone or something; on Earth, they represented the Lord. They had every advantage: a perfect home, a perfect purpose, a perfect relationship.

So *why* did they end up immobilized by temptation and neutralized by sin? *Why* did a perfect beginning degenerate into the
chaos we experience now?

Two reasons.

We're Free to Choose

God didn't create us to be automatons. Instead, the One who uttered neutrons into existence gave His greatest masterpieces the
freedom to dream, to use their imaginations, and to think on their
own. They were free to work with their hands and to create. They
were free to make their own decisions and to govern the world on
His behalf. But in doing so, the Lord exposed himself to the pain
of jilted love.[10] Adam and Eve could choose to *love* God and to
become even clearer reflections of Him . . . or they could choose
to turn their backs on Him and *reject* Him altogether.

God could have existed for all of eternity without pain, but instead He risked anguish in order to have someone outside himself
to love; someone who might freely love Him back.[11] And this is the
genius of His creation.

Karen C. Hinckley, of Yale University, explains it this way in
The Story of Stories: The Bible in Narrative Form:

> He [God] had previously made creatures who were pure spirit:
> They could reason, make choices, and perceive qualities in God
> like His majesty. "Holy, holy, holy!" they cried as they worshiped
> Him unceasingly for His greatness and perfection. But His love
> was beyond their capacity to grasp. A being needed feelings—even
> passion—to understand what it would mean to offer oneself to
> another vulnerably and to share—well, to share love. God was a
> passionate, self-giving Being, and His angels were utterly unable
> to appreciate this side of Him. On the other side, animals had

feelings but could not reason and make moral choices; their love lacked consciousness and maturity. Man was God's ingenious hybrid—spirit and soul, reason and passion, the finest reflection of Himself that God could produce.[12]

God put Adam and Eve in charge of the garden to practice their godlike qualities of creativity and authority. So they could practice their ability to make moral choices, he gave them one restriction: Don't eat from "the Tree-of-Knowledge-of-Good-and-Evil."[13]

But then an invader from outside the physical universe, a spirit who camouflaged himself as a snake, tempted Eve: "God knows that when you eat from it your eyes will be opened, and you will be like God, knowing good and evil."[14] In other words, *He doesn't really love you. He wants to keep you ignorant, under His thumb, abiding by an endless list of unreasonable rules. You're more an amusing pet than a person. Rebellion is your only choice.*

Adam and Eve had no idea that the imposter had been the highest of God's angelic servants until he himself rebelled. According to tradition, his name had been Lucifer ("lightbearer") but became Satan ("the adversary") and Abaddon ("the destroyer"). He decided he didn't want to spend eternity worshiping his Creator; he considered that to be beneath him. So he declared his independence and set up a rival kingdom.[15]

The wily serpent knew how to sway the minds of the world's first couple. *Does God really know what's best for you? Could you be happier looking out for yourselves instead of always listening to Him?*

The scent and color of the forbidden fruit enticed their senses, and suddenly everything they knew about the Lord—His desire for them, His loving care, His wisdom and gentleness—all was forgotten. At that moment, truth was traded for lies. As they gave in to temptation and were dragged into revolt, a deadly menace was freed. This lethal foe now would taunt and toy with humans until the end of time.

We Ache for Control

Deep in our heart of hearts, we all want to call the shots for ourselves.

I'm going to live my life my way—carve out my place in this world, find my meaning, and get what satisfies me. Sometimes we even mouth the lies Satan whispered in the garden: *I'm just not ready to fully trust God. I mean, how can I be sure He really cares about me and my problems? If He does, then where is He? Why can't I hear Him? Maybe I really would be happier doing things my way.*

Yet our preoccupation with *me*—and not with God—is exactly what went wrong in the garden. Adam and Eve rejected God's one single command, and all of human history changed. They bought the lie from Satan: They became convinced that being in charge of their own soul was best.

The problem with this strategy is that we humans tend to make bad choices. Part of the reason is that we don't see the entire picture, the complete story. But another reason is that, quite simply, we're selfish. Since the fall, self-centeredness—not God-centeredness—has become our defining characteristic.

"Governing the cosmos on God's behalf was and is not enough for humanity," says Scot McKnight. "Humans ache to rule the cosmos. They want to be God. The ache to be God and act as if we are God is what sin is all about."[16]

Even though there is plenty of evidence down through the ages that humankind's view of good and evil is flawed, we still want to be in control. Isn't this how most of us live our lives? Its appeal is to our baser instincts.

Nonetheless, try as we might, yearn as we do, we are *not* the master of our fate or the captain of our soul. Like it or not, sin leads us down only deadly paths, and all kinds of them:

- *We allow our will to usurp the power of God.*
- *We redefine sin and morality: "There is a way that appears to be right, but in the end it leads to death."*[17]
- *We base our significance (and the status of others) on fleeting markers like strength, beauty, intelligence, achievements, wealth.*
- *We seek happiness anywhere but the Source: alcohol and other drugs, obsessions with our own pleasures and pastimes (sports and gambling or getaways and shopping), houses, pets, possessions.*
- *We seek love anywhere but the Source: We rely on our relationships with other people, we give in to lust, we misuse sensuality and sex.*
- *We seek meaning anywhere but the Source: careers, religious practices, power.*

Think about a typical day. Much of it gets spent trying to make life work *without* God in the center. Yet we still expect Him to co-operate—relating to us on *our* terms, revolving around *our* plans, solving problems so we can live how *we* want to live. And while we may think our lives are humming along just fine, we've been deceived. Gradually, choice by choice, a chasm between us and God is growing wider and deeper.

Humming along fine? Disconnecting from the Source is disastrous.

Simply put, separation from the Lord is *the* root cause of everything that has gone wrong (and will go wrong) in our lives. It's the cause of that splinter so deeply embedded in our souls, which brings us back to the question *Why?*

> Why is it so easy to listen to the whisperings of a snake and so hard to hear the voice of the Lamb? Why are we drawn so naturally to illusion and so slow to pursue the truth? I think it's because ever since Adam and Eve's fatal choice, the jargon of temptation has been our natural tongue and the dialect of love has been a foreign language.[18]

And So We Wander Through the Desert . . .

One morning during devotions, I opened my Bible to Leviticus. *Should I read this book?* I asked myself. *Does anything in here actually apply to my life?*

Surprisingly—*yes.*

Even though you and I—along with everyone else—yearn for the garden, our sin has left us in a hostile wasteland. Cleansing the earth with a flood was a shocking way to get our attention: Humankind's inner corruption must be destroyed; holiness must be lived.[19] Yet the Ten Commandments God laid down[20] were (and are) continually broken, and His once freshly scrubbed creation again became stained, polluted by the same flaws that had earned Lucifer a place in hell: *rage, envy, gluttony, sloth, pride, lust, greed.*

Leviticus shows us that the Lord isn't giving up on humankind.

God enthroned himself right in their midst—confined behind four layers of curtains and a screened courtyard. Without the barriers, His holy presence would have disintegrated anyone who came near Him. Sin and holiness are like gasoline and fire—they simply cannot come in contact with each other.

He longed to wander among His children as He had in Eden, to look into their eyes, face-to-face again. He wanted them to be holy with Him—set apart from the world order that the Serpent's influence had perverted. So once more He had to use shocking methods to teach some shocking truths.

Seemingly endless blood sacrifices had to be brought to the Lord every day. To many contemporary ears, this sounds like senseless waste and cruelty, but God required it because the people had to learn: *Evil costs dearly.*

Whenever someone offered an animal, he laid his hands on it to identify himself with it. As he watched it butchered and burned, he knew that God was accepting its death in his place.[21]

Imagine being a priest. You'd spend your day slaughtering bulls and goats and lambs, removing hides, separating organs and fat, cutting meat into pieces. You'd be wringing doves' necks and tearing off doves' wings, and you'd be constantly sprinkling blood around on altars and toes and earlobes.

Imagine the stench—all that blood, the flies, the mess. And imagine, most of all, that it never stops. As a priest finishes with one bull, some guy comes up with another and says, "Can you please handle El Toro here? I didn't even realize I was sinning, but I just messed up."[22]

Imagine the misery. The people would keep on sinning, and the priests would keep on slicing up warm flesh.

Why this ongoing massacre? What did a human's personal life have to do with a blameless animal? *Everything.* People could not be released from sin's guilt without payment for sin's cost—remember, holiness and unholiness, or purity and impurity, cannot coexist. The only way they could be absolved was by the sacrifice of someone or something innocent of the offense.

As many lessons as the sacrificial system taught, it was not a deterrent to sin—the Old Testament is plain as day on this. The people went on sinning, and the priests went on butchering.[23]

Humans have a way of making routine that which should be startling. God's holiness demands that a price be paid for treason;

that price is death, separation from Him. But He knows that, having fallen, His people are incapable of living perfectly. For a time, for payment in blood, He accepted an animal to substitute for the human.[24]

Yet just for a time. That system was not God's ultimate plan, and it would remain in place only until the time was right for *God himself* to become the once-for-all sacrifice for sin.

The Way of the Cross

The hour had come. God the Son was about to be slain before the eyes of the world, but first the soldiers decided to have some "fun" with Him.[25]

Jesus was shredded with a whip that had multiple leather strips, each armed at the end with sharp metal or bone. Then, after His captors had woven a crown from a bush (each thorn about an inch long and sharp as a needle), one jammed it down onto His head. Another hung a purple robe on His mutilated body, and the crowd jeered at Him.

Some spat on Jesus. The soldiers made a game of punching Him in the face again and again and again as they demanded that He "prophesy" by telling them who, in turn, had struck Him.

Once Jesus was led to "the place of the skull,"[26] those who gathered at the cross beheld hate at its worst and love at its best. People so hated that they killed God's Son; God so loved that He gave people life.[27]

Iron spikes were driven completely through each of His hands and feet. He was stripped naked and raised high into the air for all to see and scorn as He hung for hours in the Middle Eastern sun. Jesus eventually became so exhausted that no matter how hard He tried, He could not hold His body up by His pierced feet. He began to hang from His torn hands, His weight gradually pulling apart His arms and shoulders.

He struggled to keep shifting back to His feet, but exhaustion gradually overtook Him until, finally, His arms bore all His weight. Thus His body began to cave in on itself as He couldn't gasp enough air into His lungs.

There, in the blistering heat—battered beyond comprehension and nearly beyond recognition, with spikes through His limbs and His bones being pulled from their sockets—Jesus slowly suffocated to death. What had been foretold hundreds of years earlier came to pass:

> He was pierced for our transgressions,
>   he was crushed for our iniquities;
> the punishment that brought us peace was on him,
>   and by his wounds we are healed.
> We all, like sheep, have gone astray,
>   each of us has turned to our own way;
> and the Lord has laid on him
>   the iniquity of us all.[28]

Onlookers witnessed even more than the fulfillment of prophecy. Nature itself began to writhe and cry out at what we were doing to our Maker.

> From noon to three, the whole earth was dark. Around midafternoon Jesus groaned out of the depths, crying loudly, "*Eli, Eli, lama sabachthani?*" which means, "My God, my God, why have you abandoned me?"
> Some bystanders who heard him said, "He's calling for Elijah." One of them ran and got a sponge soaked in sour wine and lifted it on a stick so he could drink. The others joked, "Don't be in such a hurry. Let's see if Elijah comes and saves him."
> But Jesus, again crying out loudly, breathed his last.
> At that moment, the Temple curtain was ripped in two, top to bottom. There was an earthquake, and rocks were split in pieces.

What's more, tombs were opened up, and many bodies of believers asleep in their graves were raised. (After Jesus' resurrection, they left the tombs, entered the holy city, and appeared to many.)

The captain of the guard and those with him, when they saw the earthquake and everything else that was happening, were scared to death. They said, "This has to be the Son of God!"[29]

That was true. And so was destroyed the curtain that set apart the holy from the profane, the barrier between the created and the Creator. Jesus' payment for our sins now made it possible for anyone to be made pure enough to stand in God's presence.

The Maker of the world had paid for the world's defiant disobedience. The sacrifice, the substitution for our punishment, was complete. All who have believed were—*are*—freed from the power of the deadliest menace.

Satan had lost. No matter how many battles would be waged from then to the end, the *war* with sin was *over*.

Now it was simply up to each individual to step forward and claim the victory that already had been entirely, eternally achieved.

Now it's time to fight back.

Jesus said,

This is war, and there is no neutral ground. If you're not on my side, you're the enemy; if you're not helping, you're making things worse.[30]

My Story, *Your* Story . . .

There's an ongoing tug-of-war in every heart.

As much as we long to be in control, we also yearn to get home— to our true home, with Jesus; to the everlasting garden where we'll walk with Him "in the cool of the day"[31] and "be like him, for we shall see him as he is."[32] There'll be no fear, no shame, no pain, no suffering, no hatred, and no regrets. There'll be perfect harmony: God and us—woven together in flawlessly intimate melody. *It's up to us to choose Him.*

It's up to us to release control and to surrender that ache to Him.

As God's human creations, we're free to follow a life-path that will lead us into His eternal kingdom (which promises to be unimaginably more wondrous than Eden) . . . *or* we can determine to remain in the thorns. Remember: On this battlefield, there isn't a no-man's land.

> *We can choose God's life and see manifested in us the fruits of the Spirit: love, joy, peace, forbearance, kindness, goodness, faithfulness, gentleness, and self-control.*

OR

> *We can choose our own way and yield to the acts of the sinful nature, allowing ourselves to degenerate with the cravings of the flesh: sexual immorality, impurity and debauchery, idolatry and witchcraft, hatred, discord, jealousy, fits of rage, selfish ambition, dissensions, factions, envy, drunkenness, orgies, and the like.*[33]

During my dark moments, when I find myself entangled with temptation and dragged away by sin, I've caught myself asking if I'll ever "get there."

I've made some dumb choices during my six decades on planet Earth. (And not just "long ago," either.) I've allowed that ache in my own soul to push God's authority and power right out of my life. Thankfully, though, the ache that knocks me off course from time to time also ends up dropping me to my knees in humble repentance.

I've made some good choices too.

I committed my life to Jesus Christ fourteen years ago, and every day since I've given that same heart to my beautiful wife, Char. I raised four one-of-a-kind kids. I dedicated myself to supporting and building up the church. (Researching and writing this book also falls into the "good" category!)

Regardless, the spiritual tug-of-war doesn't let up, and the apostle Paul's anguish frequently becomes mine:

> I do not understand my own actions. For I do not do what I want, but I do the very thing I hate. . . . I have the desire to do what is right, but not the ability to carry it out. For I do not do the good I want, but the evil I do not want is what I keep on doing. Now if I do what I do not want, it is no longer I who do it, but sin that dwells within me.[34]

If you're feeling alone in your win-lose battle with temptation, listen clearly: Do not allow yourself to fall victim to the enemy's "isolate and destroy" strategy. He wants you to feel as if you're the exception—a hopeless spiritual loser. The truth is you're not alone. *Every* human soul is a battleground: "Surely I was sinful at birth, sinful from the time my mother conceived me."[35] And there, in *each* of us, a war between good and evil is fought every second of every day.

Through Christ, we all can be spiritual winners as well.

Here are a few things for us to get through our heads:

We are the prodigal son.
We are Adam and Eve.
We are not alone.

God lavished upon the first humans everything they needed—every advantage to succeed. He gave them the tools to withstand temptation and to stay outside sin's grip.

He's still doing this today. The Bible proves it, and research confirms it.

◆ ◆ ◆

Now, let's roll up our sleeves and get practical! Whether you're male or female, young or old, rich or poor, we've shown you two universal truths:

1. We all struggle with temptation and sin.
2. Jesus Christ can free us from bondage to soul-robbing choices.

In the following section (and the similar section in each subsequent chapter), let us nudge you toward real change, toward true transformation! We've laid out a proven path to help you engage the Bible and hear God's personal message to you, to learn approaches to spiritual growth that are helping other believers (based on current research findings), and to chart a realistic plan for navigating any temptation trap you'll encounter.

NUDGE ONE: Learn to Be God-Centered

TEMPTED—Identifying Soul-Robbing Traps

As hard as it is to admit, here's what comes between God and me:

I know my sins have been pardoned—and I know I've been freed from their power—yet still I fall into the same traps. These are a couple of the issues at work in my heart:

I'd like Jesus to help me with . . .

TESTED—Learning How to Break Free

What research confirms about our self-centeredness and how it clouds God's purpose for our lives:

Ask several people "Why are we here?" and you're likely to get a wide range of replies, including "chance," "the Big Bang," and "reincarnation." Share this same question at church, and there's a 50/50 chance you'll get a biblically accurate response. According to Scripture, our main goal—all of us—is to bring glory to God and to find our meaning in Him. *The Westminster Catechism* (a list of questions and answers on the basics of our faith) says:

> What is the chief end of man?
> The chief end of man is to glorify God and enjoy Him forever.

Yet only half the folks sitting around you have a clear sense of what God wants from us—what His purpose is for our lives. The truth is, we've all become calloused toward and desensitized by sin, and to the degree that we're desensitized we're also confused about who we are and why we're here. We're steered by self-centered thinking. We struggle to keep our focus on God and to remain attuned to His heart, His will, His voice.

A Proven Path:

(1) Acknowledge your self-centeredness.
(2) Let Jesus move your heart toward God-centeredness.

From Genesis to Revelation, God's Word holds up a mirror to each of us. Off on our own, we're lost and miserable. But that's not how God created us to live. His design was, is, and always will be that we share His joy—that we become holy, glorifying and drawing close to Him.

Learning to become God-centered is our first crucial step. We need to put God back in His rightful position—smack in the *center* of our lives.

What Christ-Followers Are Telling Us:

It comes down to cheap grace vs. costly grace. I've been reading Dietrich Bonhoeffer's classic *The Cost of Discipleship,* which has been a real eye-opener. I must confess that I was once a believer who thought sinning was okay because, having chosen to believe in Jesus, I'm forever "covered" by His grace. Reality check: While salvation is free to us, providing it for us cost Him everything, and we're never to make light of His great sacrifice by making friends with sin and thus cheapening the grace for which He gave His life. I'm learning to take seriously my struggles and to allow Jesus to put temptation in its place. He's the one who saved me, and He himself says, "Go and sin no more."[36]

TRUE—Charting a Path Toward Change

1. *RECEIVE God's Word.* Read or listen to Hebrews 10:19–39.
2. *REFLECT on verses 26–31.* Pull them apart sentence by sentence, seeking God's personal message to you. Invite His Spirit to speak.

If we deliberately keep on sinning after we have received the knowledge of the truth, no sacrifice for sins is left, but only a fearful expectation of judgment and of raging fire that will consume the enemies of God. Anyone who rejected the law of Moses died without mercy on the testimony of two or three witnesses. How much more severely do you think someone deserves to be punished who has trampled the Son of God underfoot, who has treated as an unholy thing the blood of the covenant that sanctified them, and who has insulted the Spirit of grace? For we know him who said, "It is mine to avenge; I will repay," and again, "The Lord will judge his people." It is a dreadful thing to fall into the hands of the living God.

What is God saying to you? After a moment of silence before Him, converse with Him (talk and listen) through prayer.
Begin with general thoughts and impressions . . .

- "Heavenly Father, here's what I feel when I read these verses":

_____

- "Here's what's hard for me, God—what I don't understand":

_____

Now relate these verses to your specific struggles . . .

- "This is what Hebrews 10:19–39 is telling me about the constant *ME* focus I battle and how it can lead to sin":

_____

- "With your help, Lord, here's how I'll endeavor to overcome soul-robbing choices":

_____

3. **MEMORIZE Hebrews 10:35–36.** Repeat it to yourself as often as needed. Write it on an index card and post it where you'll see it.

Do not throw away your confidence; it will be richly rewarded. You need to persevere so that when you have done the will of God, you will receive what he has promised.

4. LISTEN to a friend. J. I. Packer says, of God's purpose for our lives:

> We were all created to be God's image-bearers. . . . We are made in such a way, I believe, that we are only at peace with ourselves when it's God's truth that our minds are grasping and consciously obeying. Human life is lacking dignity until you get to that point.[37]

5. RESPOND to God's nudges. Try this musical exercise:

- *Listen to and study* Messiah, *George Frederic Handel's symphonic masterpiece. For a truly meaningful experience, learn some details about it—look online or head to the library. One example: Handel used a technique called "text painting" (or tone painting), in which notes and scales mimic the lines of text from which the lyrics are drawn as he re-created scenes of Christ's passion, from the horrific crucifixion to the triumphant resurrection.*

- As you listen, read Matthew 27. Also, flip back and reread "The Way of the Cross" section from earlier in this chapter.

- While listening, ponder these questions:
  What emotions stir in me?
  What am I feeling about my sin . . .
  about Christ's sacrifice?
  Does Messiah *fill me with hope?*
  (Why, or why not?)

- Tap in to the power of the cross. Cooperate with God by making Christ the object of your attention, the focus of your life.[38]

- Seek to *live* the cross every day: "I want to know Christ . . . becoming like him in his death."[39] The more you see Him, the better you understand Him, and the more you'll want to die to your selfish desires, to your self-made plans, to your soul-robbing choices.

6. PRAY. Consider expressing to God this prayer by Margaret
Cundiff:

*Lord, you know me. I am so set in my ways at times. I am
stubborn, self-centered, and so sure I know it all. I must make
you angry at times. Yet you love me, you are sorry for me,
you want to give me so much. Give me the grace to admit
when I am wrong, to turn from my self and accept your love,
your way, your will.*[40]

2

The Life Cycle of a Dangerous Choice

Four Stages of Temptation

John, now a seasoned "fisher of men"[1]—wise in years, a bit slower in step—took a deep breath of sea air and surveyed the jagged coastline of Patmos.

A cloudless sky blended so seamlessly with the intense blue Aegean, he almost couldn't tell where the heavens ended and the sea began. Off to the east he spotted some hills on the Asian mainland. John closed his eyes and groaned.

Despite the beauty all around, this tiny Mediterranean paradise was only a prison—a Roman penal colony for those deemed political or religious troublemakers. And that's exactly how the empire had labeled John.

It was AD 95, and the deluded Emperor Domitian was insisting that everyone address him as *dominus et deus* ("master and god").[2] He wasn't about to abide a scruffy band of radicals who went around proclaiming the lordship of Jesus Christ. Those who challenged him ended up destitute, damaged, dead, or at best, detained.

By this time, John was the last living man who'd been intimate friends with Jesus. He'd given up everything to follow the Lord—his family and friends, his home by the Sea of Galilee, his father's lucrative business. He was willing even to lay down his life for the cause of Christ. Yet here he was, marooned on a rock, cut off from the churches in his care . . . blocked from doing the Lord's work.

Has it all been worth it?

Is heaven really in control of events down here?

Can God truly change a sinful human heart?

The Roman army had crushed Jerusalem and leveled its temple in response to a Jewish revolt.[3] Now self-proclaimed "teachers of divine truth"—false prophets, vicious wolves in sheep's clothing[4]— were confusing believers with a harmful hodgepodge: a pinch of Plato, a dash of dualism, one ancestral cult (or another) for tradition's sake . . . and then a sprinkling of Jesus into the mix.[5] Many Christians were falling for this stuff.

How can this be? The war was won on the cross—why does finding the way seem so hard? Why does sin seem to get the upper hand?

As John was about to see, two kingdoms had collided when Jesus died and rose again. Believers—*overcomers through Christ*—are on the winning side.

🍎   🍎   🍎

It was Sunday. John went to take shelter in a hillside cave, his temporary home on the island. (Today, many call it the Cave of the Apocalypse.) As he began to pray and worship God, he was startled by a loud voice behind him that sounded like a piercing trumpet: "Write on a scroll what you see. . . ."[6]

John whirled around, astonished. It was *Jesus.*

And not only the man he'd broken bread with on the shores of the Tiberias, but the One who'd showed them the holes in His hands and side.

The resurrected Lord stood before him in magnificent glory, unveiled to John's mortal eyes, glowing with divine fire. This Jesus was a stunning vision of power and judgment and awe: He was at the center of a gold menorah with seven branches. He wore a long robe with a golden sash around His chest. His head and hair were white as snow; His eyes were like flames of fire. His feet were like polished bronze; His voice "thundered like mighty ocean waves."[7]

He held seven stars in his right hand . . . from His mouth came a double-edged sword . . . His face was as bright as the sun.[8]

And it was too much for John to bear. *He fell in a dead faint at Christ's feet.*

But then Jesus placed His right hand on His apostle and said:

Don't fear: I am First, I am Last, I'm Alive. I died, but I came to life, and my life is now forever. See these keys in my hand? They open and lock Death's doors, they open and lock Hell's gates. Now write down everything you see: things that are, things about to be. . . .[9]

Jesus opened the spiritual realm to John, giving him a personal tour of heaven and showing him what needed still to happen on Earth. Unimaginable visions began to flash before his eyes—scene after scene of doom and deliverance, terror and triumph . . . a mind-boggling rush of color and sound, of image and energy, of malevolence and majesty.

Each one resounded with a single message: *"Yes, I am in control."*

🍎 🍎 🍎

The lesson John learned is as unalterably true today as it was then: Things were not as they seemed. Evil, though widespread, was not—and is not—winning. Faithfulness, though costly, was not—and is not—futile. Affliction, though continuing, most definitely will end. "The Lion's roar will soon be heard. Until then, we must reign with the Lamb."[10]

Seven times Jesus revealed how to find the path home, the narrow way.[11]

Jesus calls us to overcome!

To the one who is victorious, I will give the right to eat from the tree of life, which is in the paradise of God.[12]

The one who is victorious will not be hurt at all by the second death.[13]

To the one who is victorious, I will give some of the hidden manna. I will also give that person a white stone with a new name written on it, known only to the one who receives it.[14]

To the one who is victorious and does my will to the end, I will give authority over the nations—that one "will rule them with an iron scepter and will dash them to pieces like pottery"—just as I have received authority from my Father. I will also give that one the morning star.[15]

The one who is victorious will . . . be dressed in white. I will never blot out the name of that person from the book of life, but will acknowledge that name before my Father and his angels.[16]

The one who is victorious I will make a pillar in the temple of my God. Never again will they leave it. I will write on them the name of my God and the name of the city of my God, the new Jerusalem, which is coming down out of heaven from my God; and I will also write on them my new name.[17]

To the one who is victorious, I will give the right to sit with me on my throne, just as I was victorious and sat down with my Father on his throne.[18]

> ### *"Those who are victorious will inherit all this, and I will be their God and they will be my children."*[19]

🍎 🍎 🍎

Fast-forward a couple thousand years into the future.

Jesus still holds the keys, Satan still is defeated, and God's plan is no nearer to being frustrated now than it was then.[20] Even so, at times we all feel the frustrated powerlessness of perceiving that we assert no influence, hold no sway, and make no difference. At times we all feel isolated and stuck. There is many a day in which sin seems to be carrying it; people are as selfish and mixed up as ever; countless believers are still falling for worthless words and a harmful hodgepodge (with a little bit of Jesus sprinkled over the batch).

Yet Christ's directive is crystal clear: *Overcome.*

This brings us to a sobering question.

"How Can I Overcome Temptation?"

The verses in the Bible that tell us to "overcome" are more frustrating than comforting. The thing I don't understand is, how? I seriously *struggle* with my struggles. Willpower and good intentions just don't make them go away.

—Gina

I'm a young man who's preparing for a career in Christian ministry, yet I still act like a kid and play around with sexual temptation:

I look at pornography and I treat women like objects instead of the amazing people God created them to be. I feel pathetic and ashamed. I'm ready to get my life right. Where do I start?

—Sean

I need to "un-master" a sin that's mastering me . . . but I simply don't know how. I go several days without giving in to my habit, and then I wear down, and temptation grows stronger. Before I know it, I'm sinning again.

—B. J.

When you read Christ's calls to overcome—especially "The one who is victorious will not be hurt at all by the second death"[21]—do you find yourself at peace . . . or breaking into a cold sweat? Are you comforted . . . or agitated?

During my journalism career and ministry experience, I (Mike) have connected with hundreds of Christians who are convinced that overcoming temptation is more than a lofty goal—it's utterly unattainable. Conversely, some are convinced that they're doing nothing wrong—despite what God's Word says. Patrick A. Means, an expert on addiction recovery, says that "when we want something badly enough, we'll deceive whomever we have to in order to get it. And the first person we have to deceive is ourselves." Patrick Means observes that we accomplish the self-deceit by telling ourselves two lies:

(1) I don't really have a problem.
(2) I can handle this alone.[22]

The truth is, for *everyone* there's at least one thing that's so desirous, so attractive, that even the mere thought of it can tip us over the edge. We're spellbound by its allure; being near to it immobilizes our senses.

"That thing" seems to own us. It whispers to us. It calls out to us. And when it presents itself, we are completely undone. Scripture warns that temptation comes in many forms. Sometimes it's disguised as a lover and friend. Sometimes it appears clothed even in light, approaching with seemingly innocent intentions. Temptation is always stealthy, always deceptive . . . much like a certain snake that entered a certain garden long, long ago.

But here's a secret about our sinful desires: They're quite predictable, always attacking our minds in the same way. James—a half-brother of Jesus—knew this all too well, and he observed four stages in the temptation cycle: enticement, conception, birth, and death.

> God cannot be tempted by evil, nor does he tempt anyone; but each person is tempted when they are dragged away by their own evil desire and enticed. Then, after desire has conceived, it gives birth to sin; and sin, when it is full-grown, gives birth to death.[23]

The Birds and the Bees—and the *Birth* of Death

While an initial read of this analogy may seem a bit strange, James is personifying sin from a Hebrew perspective, referring to it as a separate being with its own existence. The ancient Jews thought that a desire—even a word—could have a life of its own. For instance, they maintained that after a word had been spoken, it could not be retrieved or reversed; it continued to move forward and become a force that, whatever strength it would bear, carried consequences people couldn't control.

For a closer look at how these "stages" apply to temptation, we're going to view them from a biological-relational angle. In other words, we're going to talk about the birds and the bees. (Bear with me, okay?)

Enticement

It starts with a pang of desire—an enthralling thought, a fantasy that perhaps, somehow, could become reality. *What if? Who would it hurt? How would it feel?* If, instead of fleeing, we entertain these thoughts for long, an "innocent pang" progresses to flirting . . . then dating . . . then eventually the decision to *commit.*

This illustrates how temptation can result in sin.

We acknowledge that we're attracted. We "run into it" at unexpected times. Eye contact and body language begin to reveal the extent of attraction and desire. We gradually move through the stages of *intimacy,* engaging sight, sound, smell, taste, touch.

Conception

Eventually our "relationship" with temptation becomes so strong that we're overwhelmed with desire for it. Foreplay leads to full consummation.

The Bible tells us that the joining of a man and a woman is not just physical but also deeply spiritual. And this unification of spirit and body can result in the formation of another being, another soul. In the case of temptation, the new being is a monster.

As we continue to engage and nurture our temptation, we choose to ignore the whispers of God. When this happens, He raises His voice. He begins to call a little louder and speak to us more firmly. He uses all kinds of methods to get our attention and to help us turn from the path we're on, to compel us to flee before sin is conceived.

Gestation and Growth

Implicit in James's analogy is that if sin is conceived in us, then, within us, it will continue to grow. If we don't heed God's warnings, we end up dragged into the next phase of the temptation cycle: We surrender to sin mentally, spiritually, and sometimes physically. We join it. We become one with it. We begin to "know" it.

Soon our "relationship" is pregnant with new possibilities that thrill us or sate us or lend us some form of comfort or escape. We love nurturing this new secret life inside us: *It is ours and ours alone.* We're convinced that no one else knows, and we hold it very close—never letting on what we're carrying inside. We nurture our sin with all the love and energy we can afford. For some, the thing that holds our desire begins to define us, giving us what we think of as our very *identity*, our very *purpose*.

We may have fleetingly considered the possibility of negative consequences, but how can we meaningfully consider the negatives when the positives have such a magnetic pull? The satisfaction we feel keeps our mind from acknowledging the long-term effects. The brain's serotonin levels increase; our pleasure and perceived happiness obviate all thought of consequences. Everything feels shiny and sweet.

Yet fantasy is hardly ever grounded in reality. Eventually, reality bites.

When a child is conceived, he's planted deeply in his mother's womb. A source of nourishment is established, a connection in "the secret place" where he can be protected and grow in a warm, dark environment, barely affected by the outside world. Two lives in one body: one outward, one hidden.

Biology thus lends insight into how we nurture temptation and grow sin. It forms within us, conceived by desire and the allure of hope for some secret happiness, pleasure, or closeness, and we allow it to be planted deep within.

Here, in the dark, we do not allow the light of truth to permeate. Here we nurture our new passion little by little, telling no one, showing no outward signs of what we've conceived. As we feed it, we grow it.

The once-miniscule sin keeps growing, taking on more strength and more life of its own. At some point we're so pregnant with sin that it begins to show. Our life begins to exhibit outward changes, and others may start to see that something has changed about us. We may alter our habits, wear different clothes, not sleep as well, or eat or drink only certain things.

We have cravings. We're feeding the sin. It's growing and growing.

Delivery

James explains that in the end, sin becomes mature. When its gestation within us is complete, it gives birth to death. Something *always* dies when sin is delivered. It may be a death inside us, or it may cause death in our family or in our world. The ugly truth is: "The wages of sin is death."[24]

The Answer: Overcome Temptation Through Christ's Power

I'm thrilled that this ugly truth has a beautiful "second half"— *"but the gift of God is eternal life in Christ Jesus our Lord."*[25] We can stop sweating and start cheering. Go ahead, let out a whoop. It's okay if people think you're crazy; this is one crazy-wonderful reality!

Jesus has the strength we lack. While we don't have the power to enact our freedom, He does.

Only His blood can wash away sin and destroy its work within us. Only His grace can break our chains and release us from the bondage that is the wages of sin. For this to happen, our "inner Frankenstein" must be put to death—along with our old self that has been chained to sin. Complete freedom comes as we become a new creation.[26] And *God* has made a way!

First, understand that *God wants everything:* our good, our bad, and our ugly. As C. S. Lewis said, and as we all must learn, no half-measures will do. As we surrender it all to Him, and Jesus begins His work in us, He digs deep into our hearts and uproots our old ways of thinking and acting. He confronts our selfish desires, our addictions, our idols, our negativity, our bitterness, our confusion—and He replaces it all. And there's more; He isn't stopping there. All along the way, through every single step, if we're willing, He'll take our hand and walk alongside us, never leaving and never rejecting us. The God who forgives, and gives, and then goes on giving and giving and giving, is *with* us all the way to our ultimate home: *eternal life with Him.*

Second, the process may feel scary at first; we may feel like resisting. But God loves us. He's always speaking to our hearts, coaxing, advising, wooing us back to the right path. He's ever seeking to infuse us with wisdom and courage to stay strong, to turn from temptation, to choose well. He whispers, "No, come away . . . avert your eyes . . . close your ears . . . put your hand over your mouth . . . think *whatever is true and kind and pure.* . . ."[27]

Third, becoming victorious over temptation requires early recognition of the conception of sin. As the old Benjamin Franklin saying goes, "An ounce of prevention is worth a pound of cure." In the process of exchanging all of our old self for all of Jesus, we find that there's room to move—we realize that by His grace, through His strength, we have the freedom to deny the urge to move forward, to turn around, to walk away . . . to *abstain.*

Finally, becoming self-aware and being honest (with self and with God) is essential—nonnegotiable. For example, the presence of anger, past wounds, confusion, or low self-confidence can create ideal conditions for temptation to take hold. The "gestational process" is affected by certain integral factors:

- *desire* for the thing that attracts us
- *exposure* to the thing that attracts us
- *access (or opportunity)* to engage with the thing that attracts us

What's more, if we engage and flirt with the attraction, our imagination (our thought processes) become involved, and we begin to rationalize why we should succumb to it. At the onset, or as quickly as we recognize what we're doing, we need to stop, cut off any momentum, and surrender ourselves instead to Christ's power so that the desire doesn't continue to be nourished (and therefore grow).

> *There just isn't room in our heart for both lies and truth. Reject Satan's falsehoods. Keep God's Word hidden in your heart.*[28]

🍏 🍎 🍏

Let him who thinks he stands take heed lest he fall. No temptation has overtaken you except such as is common to man; but God is faithful, who will not allow you to be tempted beyond what you are able [to bear], but with the temptation will also *make the way of escape*, that you may be able to bear it.[29]

Keys to Spiritual Transformation

There's no set formula for healing, restoration, and empowerment, but there are four key implements to discovering and keeping the joyous freedom God wants for us—the freedom Christ died to give us.

Step 1: Engage the Bible Daily

A relational approach to experiencing God's Word means we engage it daily—*receiving* it, *reflecting* on it, and *responding* to it. Scripture builds a proactive, protective factor within us. As we encounter His Word—chewing on it, savoring it, committing it to our hearts—we become stronger spiritually and thus increasingly are less likely to make decisions that result in soul-robbing actions. Defeating temptation involves a change in how we think.

Step 2: Receive "Touches" Throughout the Day

There are specific moments in a twenty-four-hour cycle when men and women are most vulnerable to temptation. At these critical times, a believer can be strengthened by a *scriptural touch*. A verse like Philippians 4:8, for instance, can become transformational when we ponder it and apply it to our lives. (In this case, we're instructed to meditate on those things that are *true, noble, right, pure, lovely, admirable, excellent,* and *praiseworthy*.)

Step 3: Build an Honest Relationship With God

So many of us are caught up in keeping secrets and wearing I've-got-it-all-together "happy masks" that we don't even realize our hotline to God has clogged up. Stripping away deceptive layers and experiencing the refreshing freedom that comes only from being forthright and straightforward begins as we (1) acknowledge and admit our "dark side," (2) faithfully confess our sin, and (3) learn to "live in dialogue" with our heavenly Father.

Step 4: Find Solid Community

Some call it accountability; we prefer *community*. We challenge you to (1) find a safe harbor in God's family and become real with other growing believers, and (2) discover how to "go tandem" with an encourager or two: friends who can walk alongside you, and vice versa.

NUDGE TWO: **Pinpoint Your Weaknesses**

TEMPTED—Identifying Soul-Robbing Traps

When it comes to temptation, my biggest weakness is . . .

Think hard about the people, places, moments throughout your day (thoughts and events) that tend to trigger weakness, and then finish this sentence: I feel most vulnerable when . . .

I'd like Jesus to help me with . . .

TESTED—Learning How to Break Free

What Research Confirms About Human Weakness:

- The Enemy's forces have studied our behavior since the day we were born. Evil attacks where we're most vulnerable. The easiest targets are our eyes and ears.
- The Enemy seeks to lure us into hostility toward God. He uses every kind of distraction imaginable: boredom, selfish desires, inferiority, drug abuse, doubt, fear, materialism, etc.
- The Enemy has an ally: our own flesh. This is the fallen-nature dimension of our life that instinctively wants to live independently from God. Even after we have committed our lives to Christ, Satan appeals to our flesh, tempting us to return to our old ways of thinking and choosing and acting.[30]

A Proven Path:

(1) Identify your weaknesses.
(2) Create a strategy to begin strengthening them.

To overcome sin, we're to consider ourselves dead to it and alive in God.

Do not let sin reign in your mortal body so that you obey its evil desires. Do not offer any part of yourself to sin as an instrument of wickedness, but rather offer yourselves to God as those who have been brought from death to life; and offer every part of yourself to him as an instrument of righteousness. For sin shall no longer be your master, because you are not under the law, but under grace.[31]

What Christ-Followers Are Telling Us:

The sins I give in to make me sick, but when temptation presents itself, it seems so attractive. I started opening up to a friend about my struggles, which is very helpful—at least for a few weeks. But as time goes by, I end up getting weak and giving in again. It's a never-ending cycle that's hard to break out of.

There's a certain sin that I can't seem to beat. As often as I promise God I won't stumble, a few days later, my strength evaporates—and I end up doing the same things over and over again. I feel like the apostle Paul: "What I want to do I do not do, but what I hate I do."[32] I want freedom from temptation, yet I feel as if I'm in a big hole . . . and I keep digging in deeper.

I can't take back control over my mind. Thoughts about certain temptations enter my head all the time. I feel so weak and so guilty about the stuff in my brain. I'm sick of living this way. I want help. I want change!

TRUE—Charting a Path Toward Change

1. *RECEIVE God's Word.* Read or listen to 1 John 2:28–3:10.
2. *REFLECT on verses 3:7–9.* Pull them apart sentence by sentence, seeking God's personal message to you. Invite His Spirit to speak.

Dear children, do not let anyone lead you astray. The one who does what is right is righteous, just as he is righteous. The one who does what is sinful is of the devil, because the devil has been sinning from the beginning. The reason the Son of God appeared was to destroy the devil's work. No one who is born of God will continue to sin, because God's seed remains in them; they cannot go on sinning, because they have been born of God.

What is God saying to you? After a moment of silence before Him, converse with Him (talk and listen) through prayer.

Begin with general thoughts and impressions . . .

- "Heavenly Father, here's what I feel when I read these verses":

- "Here's what's hard for me, God—what I don't understand":

Now relate these verses to your specific struggles.

- "Here's what 1 John 2:28–3:10 is telling me about facing my weaknesses in order to steer clear of temptation":

- "With your help, Lord, here's how I'll endeavor to overcome soul-robbing choices":

3. MEMORIZE 1 John 3:2–3. Repeat it to yourself as often as needed. Write it out on an index card and post it where you'll see it.

We know that when Christ appears, we shall be like him, for we shall see him as he is. All who have this hope in him purify themselves, just as he is pure.

4. LISTEN to a friend. Elouise Renich Fraser says our bodies can help us keep an eye on our weaknesses and stay in touch with our mental state:

My body, once ignored and despised, has become an ally in the reorientation of my internal and external life. It lets me know when

I'm running away, avoiding yet another of God's invitations to look into my past and the way it binds me as a theologian. I can't trust my mind as often as I trust my body. My mind tries to talk me into business as usual, but my body isn't fooled. Insomnia, intestinal pain, and diarrhea let me know there's work to be done.[33]

5. *RESPOND to God's nudges.* Try this exercise for help in pinpointing your vulnerability-temptation connection:

- One of my (Mike's) weaknesses is stress, which, among other things, can lead to temptations to worry and to fear. Referencing one weakness you listed above, log the moments throughout the day when you feel most vulnerable to that temptation. Do this on your "Spiritual Weakness Chart" (sample below). Write in these four pieces of information: (1) time of day, (2) place, (3) circumstances, and (4) emotions. Do this for seven consecutive days.

MY SPIRITUAL WEAKNESS CHART
When Mike Feels Most Vulnerable to the Temptation of Worry

Day	Time of Day	Place	Circumstances	Emotions
Monday	9 a.m.	Work	Meeting with peers, consultant	Fear, worry
Tuesday	7 p.m.	Home office	as I worked on family budget	Stress, fear
Wednesday	11 p.m.	Home— in bed	Troubles sleeping; thinking about deadline	Anxiety, worry
Thursday	9 a.m.	Work	Working on project; striving to meet deadline	Stress, anxiety
Friday	6 p.m.	Home	Movie night with family	Content, at peace, joyful
Saturday	9 a.m.	Home	Breakfast with wife	Relaxed, joyful
Sunday	8 p.m.	Home	Watching news	Stressed

- Turn to Worksheet 1 ("My Spiritual Weakness Chart," at end of the book) for a full-size chart you can duplicate and use.

- After the seven days, note what you have observed and choose the steps you'll take to begin making a difference.

Here's how my weaknesses triggered temptation:

Here's how the temptation gave birth/could have given birth to sin:

Here are some steps I'll take to manage my weaknesses, circumvent temptation, and overcome soul-robbing choices:

Scripture to Engage:

Issue for Prayer:

A Support Person:

Healthy Self-Talk:

---

*At www.tempted.goTandem.com, learn
how you can have Scripture delivered to
you (through phone calls, emails, text
messages) during the moments when you
feel weakest and most vulnerable. You can
also receive a weekly phone call from a
spiritual-growth encourager who will listen
and pray with you about your struggles.*

---

6. *PRAY.* Consider expressing this version of the Lord's Prayer by John Bunyan:

"Our Father which in heaven art,
Thy name be always hallowed;
Thy kingdom come, thy will be done;
Thy heavenly path be followed:
By us on earth, as 'tis with thee,
We humbly pray;
And let our bread us given be
From day to day.
Forgive our debts, as we forgive
Those that to us indebted are;
Into temptation lead us not;
But save us from the wicked snare.
The kingdom's thine, the power too,
We thee adore;
The glory shall be thine
For evermore.[34]

3

Everyday Enticements

From "Fantasy Island" to the "Gossip Graveyard"

Sarah saw everything that the family had ferried from the dinner table to the island counter. *Another load.* Those two words felt heavier than all the dishes and flatware combined. Just the thought of washing those grimy plates and pots *again* made her heart sink.

Her eyes glazed over. *I deserve a break,* she thought. *Day in and day out, start to finish, it's the same thing. I NEED DOWNTIME. I'll get to this later.*

She went around the corner, closed the den's shade, spied the remote, dropped onto the couch, flicked on the TV, and morphed into absorption.

The heirloom clock by the wall chimed. When it did so a second time, she leaned deeper into the couch and absentmindedly arranged three pillows to keep the big timepiece from lurking in her peripheral vision.

The garage door opened and then closed as her husband, John, walked into and across the house, keys jangling. "Turned into a longer meeting than planned," he said, leaning down to plant a kiss. "But at least everyone left satisfied. That's not always—" he stopped and looked up, distracted by noise from upstairs. "The girls still awake?"

"Yeah." She yawned, then stretched. "Remember? Your turn to give baths tonight?" She blinked twice, hoping he *wouldn't* remember.

He looked thoughtful. "Okay. Well, I did it last night. And Monday . . ." He paused, but then, wanting to avoid a confrontation, he quickly added, "No problem, I'll run up right now."

"Thanks, honey." Sarah turned back to her show.

🍎 🍎 🍎

The children were soon bathed and dried, brushed and tucked in.

A couple hours later Sarah moved slowly from couch to bed. She picked a novel off the nightstand and snuggled up for more downtime, telling herself she'd be back on the ball in the morning. It was long past midnight when she set down her page-turner.

🍎 🍎 🍎

The annoying sunlight persisted in leaking through the blinds. Sarah snoozed the alarm a few times, then finally just turned it off. Eventually she heard a voice ringing in her ears.

"Mommy? Mommy! It's time for school!"

She yawned and rubbed her eyes. She turned to see her first- and second-grade daughters in their pajamas, pulling on her comforter. "What time is it?" she managed to ask.

"Almost nine," announced Chloe, the elder.

Sarah shot upright at this dreadful news and hurtled into her closet. The household briefly moved into whirlwind mode as she hastily dressed the girls, rushed them into the car, raced over to the elementary school, and her heart pounding, stepped into the administration office to sign slips for the early morning doctor's appointments she'd "forgotten to clear beforehand."

🍎 🍎 🍎

Back at home, Sarah looked around the living room, cluttered with toys, and winced at seeing the table, decorated with Cheerios and milk puddles.

She took a deep sigh. She began to add the breakfast clutter to the pile on the island. But then her fatigued indifference returned. She sighed again, closed her eyes . . . and said to herself, *I just need to get away from this awhile—just to regroup. It'll be easier to face this afternoon.*

She walked out the door for some downtime at the coffee shop.

Sin Spin and Distorted Realities

Sarah struggles with sloth. You might too, or you may struggle with something else. Regardless, we all face temptation, and at one point or another we've all done what she's doing—make our sin sound "not so bad."

We tell ourselves why our choices are okay, even if "that voice" inside says they're wrong. Of course, we all *do* need downtime, breaks, and help from our spouses. But we also *do* need to take care of our responsibilities.

What we find in Sarah's justifications is exactly what we would expect: a compelling argument. Who among us tries to convince ourselves that some sin is acceptable by forging a half-baked excuse?

No, we use every bit of our rational ability, our reasoning skill, to sell our plan to the jury in our heads.

What we usually don't realize is that when we do this over and over, we start to believe our own justifications and cease to recognize our sin for what it is. That's why the prophet Jeremiah says, "The heart is deceitful above all things and beyond cure. Who can understand it?"[1] Our hearts are sin-sick, and we twist things in our minds to where we even deceive ourselves about the wickedness in our souls. We've been committed to evading the truth.

The truth, though, is that many believers have become calloused to common temptations and have cozied up to everyday sins. Let's take a look at a couple of these sins and their disguises.

Gossip

Whether we call it girl talk, guy time, shooting the breeze, or catching up on the latest, gossip is one of the sins we most readily excuse. We almost never call out our gossip for what it is. Either we joke about it, as if it were feathery-light (rather than leaden-heavy), or we veil it with the supposed reasons why we need to know—and share, sometimes as "prayer requests"—the secrets or struggles of others, whether or not the stories are true.

One way we justify gossip is by telling ourselves we need to analyze the bad decisions people make so we don't repeat their mistakes. But we're slow to admit that we derive pleasure from talking and hearing about others' problems (at their expense) because it makes us feel "better" somehow.

Gossip is serious, and there's nothing harmless about it—in fact, gossip leaves wreckage in its wake: "A whisperer separates close friends."[2] We shouldn't even "associate with a gossip,"[3] and anytime we're tempted to think God has no issue with talking about others behind their backs, we ought to remember that it shows up in a number of New Testament vice lists—short summaries of stuff we're to avoid no matter what.[4] The Bible condemns gossip because it breaks trust and tears apart all kinds of relationships—from marriages and friendships to office teams and churches.

Materialism

Materialism subsists in the very drinking water of Western culture. We're surrounded by it, immersed in it; most of us usually don't even realize when it's subtly tempting us to partake of its privileges and pleasures.

Some of us exhibit materialistic addiction when we grasp at extra stuff—another new outfit ("It's so perfect, my *name* should have been on the tag!"), more books online ("They were such a bargain, it would have been a sin *not* to get them"), more toys to top our children's overflowing bins ("They get *so* bored when there's no excitement"). Some of us feel we must have the latest gadget—the newest smartphone, the next-version tablet or SmartPad, the widest flat-screen. Some of us can't live without another latte, or dinner out, or tub or tube or box or bag of whatever it is we crave to overeat.

Some of us even get spiritual about it, reminding ourselves and others that when God's Word defines one of the roots of evil, it distinguishes between money and the *love* of money.[5] This distinction itself is important, but materialism shows its colors when we tell ourselves that we're okay because we don't actually love money—even as we're pursuing with abandon all we can possibly buy and acquire . . . or finding yet another way to get more and more of what we think we want but don't truly need.

One of the reasons materialism is so hard to pinpoint is that everyone seems to have a different notion of what passes for it. We can always look at someone who has more than we do, or tries to get more than we're trying to get, and tell ourselves we're "not as bad as them." All objects of temptation are temporal, but different people struggle with different temptations, and that makes it difficult to identify materialism consistently or categorically.

That's why we must recognize that at its heart, materialism is a state of the soul, not our state at the store. God says we're to put our money (our "treasure") where our "heart" is,[6] and our mind also should be set "on things above, not on earthly things,"[7] but if we're pursuing *stuff*, then we're wrapped up with this world—we're binding ourselves to the here and now. Such entanglement hampers our devotion to the Lord; it distracts us from ministry opportunities and increasingly closes us to God's priorities.

When we pour our time and money into fleeting goods and pleasures, we slump toward the earth and forget that "our citizenship is in heaven."[8] And as long as the earth grips our hearts, our hearts aren't laying up imperishable treasure in eternity, where we'll live forever, but rather are clawing for tokens and trinkets that "moths and vermin destroy" or "thieves break in and steal."[9]

A Pervasive Pattern

We gloss over all kinds of sin in our lives. Sometimes we put relationships, jobs, possessions, or hobbies between us and God, but instead of calling them *idols,* we call them *priorities* or *needs.* Sometimes we lie about why we're late for work or why one of our children is staying home from school, but we call it PR spin or embellishing the truth. We're lying to ourselves! *All* sin deteriorates our closeness to God and others and desiccates our own souls.

We do ourselves a disservice when we minimize what we consider "small sins" or "white lies" and fail to account for temptation's powerful sting. In his treatise "On Temptation," the seventeenth-century Puritan John Owen observed "how full is the world" of those who have fallen into temptation and then proceeded into great sin and death. He thus charged,

> Is it not time for us to awake before it be too late—to watch against the *first rising* of sin, the first attempts of Satan, and all ways whereby he hath made his approaches to us, be they never so harmless in themselves?[10]

Temptation can seem harmless on the surface, or we may *tell* ourselves it is harmless. But succumbing to temptation leads into destructive consequences, and so our most careful diligence is required to identify it, speak honestly about it, and resist it from its very "first rising" in our lives.

Many centuries ago, the church described seven particular sins as deadly or capital sins. The term *capital* comes from the Latin *caput*, meaning "head," and it indicates that these are "source sins." They're especially lethal in that they lead to many other sins, as if they were the head of a sin stream.[11]

In fact, all the so-called "smaller" sins we commit are manifestations of these deeper sin issues residing in our hearts. They're not deadly because God's grace is insufficient to cover them. They're deadly because (1) they constitute the core sinfulness that feeds our sinful thoughts and acts—the sins we commit day to day—and because (2) if they aren't dealt with, they will plunge us into spiritual death and eternal separation from God.

Many believers find it helpful to reflect on the "Seven Deadly Sins" (or the "Seven Deadlies")—*pride, envy, anger, greed, sloth, lust,* and *gluttony*—and to seek biblical guidance in overcoming temptation toward them. In this context, it will be beneficial for us to explore what they all have in common.

What Makes Sin "Deadly"

Under the Radar

First, these sins lurk beneath the surface, disguising themselves in forms we deem more acceptable. While none of us wants to call ourselves lustful or lazy, we cover up these sins with names that make them sound less dreadful.

For example, we may disguise our pride by calling it self-confidence. Greed can cloak itself all along the path to what we might call "improving our lot in life." We might call gluttony "a healthy appetite," say our envy is only "a desire for self-betterment," and justify our inner rage as "righteous indignation" or "frustration anyone would have if they'd been in my shoes."

When we excuse sins like gossip and materialism, we're really making peace with the deadly sins that give rise to our everyday iniquities. Gossip arises from our arrogance, thinking ourselves better than others, and from our envy, a sinister wish that if I can't have what she has, then she shouldn't enjoy it either. Materialism stems from greed, lust, and gluttony—our cravings and demands to obtain pleasure from temporal, material things.

"The Seven Deadlies" reveal how desperate our situation is: We deceive ourselves and dress up our sin—at all levels—to look like an acceptable or even affirmable part of our lives rather than the decaying disease it really is.

Dissatisfaction With God

Second, these sins all represent the prioritizing of our flawed passions over God's promises of true fulfillment. The degree to which we entertain and serve them is the degree to which we disbelieve and reject the truth of His Word. In harboring any of these sins, we say to God, "Not your will, but *mine* be done." Asserting our own fallen will against His is acting as if *His* purpose is somehow faulty, somehow designed to deprive us of "our happiness."

Pride itself illustrates this clearly. God gave Adam and Eve a single restraint,[12] not to deprive them but *for their good.* Yet when they chose to defy God, they (1) accused Him of withholding something good from them and (2) decreed that creatures know better than their Creator. Whenever we fail to trust God, we commit the same sin of pride.

In sloth we question the goodness of work, which God instituted *before* the fall.[13]

In lust we doubt the sufficiency of sex within a lifetime commitment.

In greed we reject the measure of "enough" and pursue the accumulation of "more."

In envy we despise God's providence and sovereignty in giving us and our neighbor different lots.

In gluttony we throw aside self-control and embrace indulgence.

In anger we proclaim that we reject how God is permitting our lives to turn out.

Essentially, in each deadly sin, we proclaim our dissatisfaction with how God calls us to live and, ultimately, with God himself. And in each, we declare that we, not God, have the truth of what it means to be happy and fulfilled.

Racing to Dead Ends

Third, these sins constitute our doomed attempts to satisfy our deepest longings with earthly pleasures or through earthly means.

This has never worked. It never will work.

In this endeavor, our true desires—the ones with which God designed us—are twisted from substance into shadow. They become misshapen and perverted as we allow sin to mask what they really are with what, more and more, we come to think and believe they are.

Instead of abiding in Jesus,[14] in place of drawing nearer to God,[15] rather than eating and drinking the Bread and Water of Life,[16] we try to satisfy or numb what are actually spiritual needs through fame and power (pride), bigger houses and better gadgets (greed), pornography and sexual self-centeredness (lust), keeping up with or outdoing our peers (envy), overindulgence of food and alcohol (gluttony), or excessive entertainment and relaxation (sloth).

Then when these fail to satisfy, we become bitter or enraged, and we're icy toward others, or we lash out and harm them emotionally, spiritually, and/or physically (anger). In our obsession with a here-today-gone-tomorrow world, we're increasingly desperate to prove that these things can and will fill a void only God can fill and slake a thirst only God can quench.

C. S. Lewis captures our myopic and ill-fated tendency to fix our affections on this world and obsess over its allurements.

> *"If we consider the unblushing promise of reward and the staggering nature of the rewards promised in the Gospels, it would seem that Our Lord finds our desires, not too strong, but too weak. We are half-hearted creatures, fooling about with drink and sex and ambition when infinite joy is offered us, like an ignorant child who wants to go on making mud pies in a slum because he cannot imagine what is meant by the offer of a holiday at the sea. We are far too easily pleased."*[17]

Only in Christ will our longings find true and complete fulfillment. And once we experience this divine contentment, we're wise
to realize we must continue seeking and finding our peace and joy
and satisfaction *in Him*: "This world in its present form is passing
away."[18] There's no other way, and nothing else even compares. We'll
discover what we're meant for in living for God, in "glorify[ing]
Him and enjoy[ing] Him forever."[19] We'll realize what matters,
what's lasting, *and* what we really want in embracing Paul's motto:

To live is Christ, and to die is gain.[20]

Turning From Sin at the Start

The Seven Deadly Sins remind us just how prone we are to sin. But
we can stop sin's flow when we recognize that *every temptation is
a life-shaping moment.* Philip Howard noted:

> The lightest inclination toward an act which is not wholly clean
> may be the real pivot on which [a person's] whole being turns just
> then and for all time. As he chooses then, so he may come to be.[21]

Every choice makes us who we are.
That's why *"every temptation is worth a fight to the death."*[22]

This means that every time we justify a sin as "small," we weaken
our defenses against all sin. Conversely, every time we turn from
even the so-called smallest of sins, we build up our resistance to
sin's patterns, which seek to seize, consume, and destroy us.

Most of all, we must know and never forget that our hope of
overcoming temptation lies not in ourselves but in Christ's power
at work in us. Dietrich Bonhoeffer placed every temptation in
the world into one of two categories: "Either the Adam in me is

tempted—in which case we fall. Or the Christ in us is tempted—in which case Satan is bound to fall."[23] Adam failed at the decisive moment and led all of humanity into sin; however, Christ "in every respect has been tempted as we are, yet without sin."[24] As He resisted every temptation, so through His death and resurrection He applies that overcoming power to His body, the church. Only by appropriating His strength can we—and we *can*—overcome the deadly sin in our lives.

The Unpardonable Sin and You: Advice From Mahesh and Bonnie Chavda

People often wonder as they begin their walk with God if they have somehow blasphemed Him. They worry about having committed the "unpardonable sin" and grieving Him beyond repair. Matthew 12:31–37 shows us clearly that this happens when we deliberately and knowingly attribute satanic action to the Holy Spirit of God. Giving the devil credit for God's work leads to blasphemy against the Holy Spirit. In many decades of dealing with human problems we have never personally encountered anyone who has committed the unpardonable sin, though we have helped to comfort and instruct a number of persons who thought they had unwittingly done so.

When the blood of Jesus was shed, it made provision for us to be born again and be rid of that innate, guilty conscience that we inherited as descendants of Adam. It is safe to say that, other than stumbling and falling into some kind of royal mess-up, guilt is the biggest barrier to walking in absolute liberty in the Holy Spirit. It is the biggest block to moving His power.

Guilt comes from a sense of having broken God's law, but remember: Condemnation is pseudo-guilt. The Holy Spirit convicts of sin. He never condemns. It is the devil who accuses, the flesh that condemns.[25]

John Wesley's Self-Examination Exercise

(1) Am I consciously or unconsciously creating the impression that I'm better than I really am? In other words, am I a hypocrite?

(2) Am I honest in all my acts and words, or do I exaggerate?

(3) Am I a slave to dress, friends, work, or habits?

(4) Did the Bible live in me today?

(5) Am I enjoying prayer?

(6) Do I disobey God in any way?

(7) Am I defeated in any part of my life?

(8) Am I jealous, impure, critical, irritable, touchy, or distrustful?

(9) Am I proud?

(10) Is there anyone whom I fear, dislike, disown, criticize, hold resentment toward, or disregard? If so, what am I doing about it?

(11) Do I grumble or complain constantly?

(12) Is Christ real to me? [26]

NUDGE THREE: Reconsider Holiness

TEMPTED—Identifying Soul-Robbing Traps

I too have justified certain sins as "small," including:

_____

_____

Of the "Seven Deadlies," the ones I think I'm most vulnerable to are:

_____

_____

Here's how I define the word *holiness*:

_____

_____

I'd like Jesus to help me with:

_____

_____

_____

TESTED—Learning How to Break Free

What Research Confirms About Disinterest in Holiness:

Many Christians believe that, because of Christ's sacrifice on the cross, sin is somehow wrapped into (and therefore cancelled out by) grace. In other words, in this view, one would say, "Of course everybody sins," and then do nothing about it. According to Scot McKnight, for many today, "sin is not only an assumption—it is an accepted assumption. And not only is it an accepted assumption—it also doesn't seem to matter."[27]

McKnight has observed, and research confirms, that widespread apathy toward sin reveals itself in our lack of interest in holiness. Why? Perhaps in some part as a reaction to the "overdoing it" of past generations. For instance, many Christians in the 1950s condemned everything from movies and rock music to dancing and drinking any alcohol. Yet while they came across as legalistic and judgmental, by contrast, many in the 1960s embraced an I-can-do-as-I-please-because-of-God's-grace attitude. That generation's lack of zeal for holiness produced a counter-trend: acceptance of sin, ignorance of its impact, and weakened relationships with God, other believers, and the world. "We are in a dangerous place today," McKnight warns. "We need to confront again the message of the Bible about sin."[28]

A Proven Path:

(1) Know what holiness is and isn't.

(2) Know that the Spirit of Christ seeks to grow holiness in each of us.

Hand in hand with God's grace and forgiveness, we need to embrace His requirement that we become holy, just as He is.[29] However, this is something that, rather than fear, can bring *joy* to our hearts. Said Oswald Chambers:

If Jesus Christ is going to regenerate me, what is the problem He faces? It is simply this—I have a heredity in which I had no say or decision; I am not holy, nor am I likely to be; and if all Jesus Christ can do is tell me that I must be holy, His teaching only causes me to despair. But if Jesus Christ is truly a regenerator, someone who can put His own heredity of holiness into me, then I can begin to see what He means when He says that I have to be holy.[30]

What Christ-Followers Are Telling Us:

I feel like Christians are so uptight about so many issues. I step into church and all I hear are sermons about sin, damnation, and holiness. What about grace? Jesus forgave us when He went to the cross. Shouldn't that be our focus?

I rarely hear about sin these days. It's almost as if my pastor is afraid to talk about it—like maybe he thinks he might offend someone. As for holiness, most people in my church—especially young people—say, "What's that?"

My church's Bible study has been talking about defeating temptations. I was thinking today, if we have a temptation and fall into it, God will forgive us. What, then, would keep us from using that as an excuse? When considering whether to do the right or the wrong thing, you could just say, "Oh, God will forgive me, so why not?"

TRUE—Charting a Path Toward Change

1. *RECEIVE God's Word.* Read or listen to Romans 6:15–23.
2. *REFLECT on verses 15–16.* Pull them apart sentence by sentence, seeking God's personal message to you. Invite His Spirit to speak.

Shall we sin because we are not under the law but under grace? By no means!

Don't you know that when you offer yourselves to someone as obedient slaves, you are slaves of the one you obey—whether you are slaves to sin, which leads to death, or to obedience, which leads to righteousness?

What is God saying to you? After a moment of silence before Him, converse with Him (talk and listen) through prayer.
Begin with general thoughts and impressions . . .

- "Heavenly Father, here's what I feel when I read these verses":

- "Here's what's hard for me, God—what I don't understand":

Now relate these verses to your specific struggles:

- "Here's what Romans 6:15–23 is telling me about the way I treat sin and sometimes neglect holiness":

- "With your help, Lord, here's how I'll endeavor to resist temptation and sin":

3. *MEMORIZE Romans 6:18.* Repeat it to yourself as often as needed. Write it out on an index card and post it where you'll see it.

> You have been set free from sin and have become slaves to righteousness.

4. *LISTEN to a friend.* Jerry Bridges says, about the pursuit of holiness:

> Prayer is a vital part of our fellowship with God; yet the psalmist said, "If I regard wickedness in my heart, the Lord will not hear" (Psalm 66:18). To regard wickedness is to cherish some sin, to love it to the extent that I am not willing to part with it. I know it is there, yet I justify it in some way like the child who says, "Well, he hit me first." When we are holding on to some sin, we are not pursuing holiness and we cannot have fellowship with God.[31]

5. *RESPOND to God's nudges.* Try this exercise in holiness:

- Conduct an impromptu "man-on-the-street"-style interview at church or in a small group. Ask five random people to define holiness—without looking at their Bibles. Jot down their answers:

      Definition 1: _____
      Definition 2: _____
      Definition 3: _____
      Definition 4: _____
      Definition 5: _____

- Compare what you heard with what the Bible says about holiness:

> Since we have these promises, dear friends, let us purify ourselves from everything that contaminates body and spirit, perfecting holiness out of reverence for God.[32]

> Make every effort to live in peace with everyone and to be holy; without holiness no one will see the Lord.[33]

As obedient children, do not conform to the evil desires you had
when you lived in ignorance. But just as he who called you is holy, so
be holy in all you do; for it is written: "Be holy, because I am holy."[34]

- Consider reading (or rereading) one of the most highly re-
  garded books on the subject: *The Pursuit of Holiness* by
  Jerry Bridges. But take it slow—like several weeks or even
  a couple months—and savor this resource. This one isn't
  meant to be a quick read.

- Write out a prayer to God, asking Him to nurture in you a
  healthy understanding of holiness—and a passion to pursue
  it:

6. PRAY. Consider expressing this prayer by John Calvin:

*O Lord God, eternal and almighty Father, we acknowledge
and sincerely confess before your holy majesty that we are
miserable sinners, conceived and born in iniquity and sin,
prone to evil, and incapable of any good work, and that
in our depravity we make no end of breaking your holy
commandments. We thus call down destruction on ourselves
from your just judgments. Nevertheless, O Lord, we lament
that we have offended you, and we condemn ourselves and
our faults with true repentance, asking you to help us from
wretchedness by your grace.*

*Deign, then, O most gracious and most merciful God and
Father, to bestow your mercy on us in the name of Jesus Christ
your Son our Lord. Effacing our faults, and all our sinfulness,
daily increase in us the gifts of your Holy Spirit that we from
our inner hearts, acknowledging our sin, may be more and
more displeasing to ourselves, and become truly repentant,
and that your Holy Spirit may produce in us the fruits of
righteousness and holiness, through Jesus Christ, our Savior.*[35]

4

Men at the Cross

Our Research Reveals Struggles Men Face

I have spent the better part of twenty years being angry at God for the death of my mother when I was nineteen, and this has become the focus of my life—to be mad.

—Keith

I think my most consistent failure is lust. I've never had a problem with infidelity, promiscuity, or pornography, but at the same time this sin itself can be very habitual because it comes from the core of the flesh. It's almost a daily fight. I want to instill in my four young boys a different moral code than my dad gave me.

—Tony

I thought drug addiction was the most difficult temptation, but I was delivered from two decades of that several years ago. Now I'm finding out there are other things I have a harder time giving to God. I worry about my wife and have a fear of abandonment. To "let go" of my wife seems to be harder than to let go of drug addiction. It's starting to get me in trouble.

—Pete

I've been looking at pornography and entertaining sexual fantasies, and fulfilling them, since I was thirteen. And though I've been able to keep it under extreme control, I still ask God why He won't make it go away and why it isn't a part of His will for my life to make it disappear. Why does GOD allow Satan to have such an unfair advantage over a much weaker human being? This addiction may be "my thorn in the side" for the rest of MY life!

—Matt

On an average day, what trips *you* up? What keeps *you* from moving closer to Jesus?

Over the past few years, I (Arnie) and my research colleague Pam Ovwigho have asked tens of thousands of people, from all walks of life, all about their daily temptations. Tens of thousands have candidly shared what tempts them, when they feel tempted, how temptation affects their spiritual life, what helps them deal with temptation . . . if you can articulate it, we've probably asked about it.

That so many have been willing to let us connect with a part of them that's typically private and heavily guarded is remarkable. Almost everyone would agree that, socially, temptation is *not* a topic of "polite conversation."

We may admit, again, that we can identify with Paul's lament: "I don't really understand myself, for I want to do what is right, but I don't do it. Instead, I do what I hate."[1] We agree, on a general level, that we struggle with desire to do what we shouldn't. Yet how truly open are we about our actual vulnerability, even with those closest to us?

Maybe you can relate to Margo from Houston, who often feels tempted to yearn for the things that others have. She said, of sharing her struggles:

> I usually regret it, because I then feel like I'm not understood or am then more vulnerable. I've been betrayed too many times in the past. That's why prayer is so predominant in my life.

Doug, from Kansas, has a similar dilemma regarding pornography:

> I haven't spoken to anyone in anything but broad "many have this problem" ways. I'm too embarrassed to talk about this to someone I personally know. I did in the past, and it ultimately yielded a divorce. So I'm no longer willing to trust anyone with my "secret." The woman who vowed to love me "till death do us part" parted ways with me when I revealed to her my weakness.

Embarrassment, the fear of being judged, or pain from past betrayal or rejection can hold us back from seeking out the counsel of others. This lack of connection, in turn, keeps us hurting and disheartened, isolated, in a bubble. It deprives us of the support and

> *encouragement that could help us triumph*
> *over temptation. And it fools us into thinking*
> *we're the only ones who are struggling.*

The reality differs dramatically from these lies Satan would have us believe. Though we try to hide it, among Christ-followers, temptation is universal and daily. Let's take a look at some of what has been shared with us:

- Four of five people will face at least one temptation in a given day.
- Men encounter twice as many occurrences of temptation as women.
- A typical experience of being tempted lasts seven to ten minutes.
- Most people give in to at least one temptation each day.
- The average Christian feels spiritually stalled four months out of the year.

Hopefully these facts will help you breathe a little easier. *You are not alone in your temptations.* Your fellow Christ-followers have many of the same struggles.

Further, feeling tempted doesn't mean you're spiritually weak— it means you're still living in and being affected by a sinful world. Experiencing temptation does not mean you aren't being transformed by the Spirit of Christ living within you, it just means that you're somewhere along the way toward the perfection to which God has called you.

🍎   🍎   🍎

There are significant differences between the temptations men and women generally encounter. Here in chapter 4 we'll examine hot-button issues for men; in chapter 5 we'll consider the primary issues for women.

Hot Button #1: The Perilous Pandemic of Sexual Temptation

We started our research with open-ended questions. For example, when we asked, "What are the three most common temptations you face?" we let people answer in their own words, with no categories or constraints. This approach gave us the widest possible portrait and didn't limit responses.

The figure to the right gives a word picture of how men answered, and one theme jumps out immediately. Across the board, across generations, across social strata, men said that temptations related to sex are the most common. In fact, three out of five Christian men name lust or pornography as their top temptation.[2]

All available evidence points to strong sexual desires and urges as a universal reality among men. Part of the reason is biological: Men are wired with a much stronger sex drive than women. Yes, there are exceptions—some men have a low sex drive and some women are on the high end. On average, though, men think more than women about sexual pleasure.

One review of the research on this topic concluded:

> Across many different studies and measures, men have been shown
> to have more frequent and more intense sexual desires than women,
> as reflected in spontaneous thoughts about sex, frequency and
> variety of sexual fantasies . . . willingness to forego sex, initiating
> versus refusing sex, making sacrifices for sex, and other measures.
> No contrary findings (indicating stronger sexual motivation among
> women) were found. Hence we conclude that the male sex drive is
> stronger than the female sex drive.[3]

Author Edward Laumann notes that the majority of men under
age sixty think about sex at least once a day. Only one in four
women report thoughts this frequent.[4]

A natural predisposition isn't the only explanation for the strong
pull of sexual temptation for men. As they navigate their day, men
encounter—intentionally or unintentionally—more sights or images that can arouse their sexual desire. In particular, the lure and
availability of Internet pornography is carving a massive path of
destruction among men, their families, and the church. Consider
these sobering statistics (as of 2010):

- One-third of Internet users have experienced unwanted exposure to pornographic content.[5]
- Seventy percent of young adult men (ages eighteen to twenty-four) visit pornographic websites in a typical month.[6]
- Each second, $3,075.64 is being spent on pornography, and 28,258 Internet users are viewing porn.[7]
- One-fourth of youth (ages ten to seventeen) using the Internet had one or more exposures to unwanted sexual images in the past year.[8]
- In 2006 there already were sixty-eight million Internet searches for pornographic material daily. This represented 25 percent of all daily search engine requests.[9]

- In 2006 forty million adults in the U.S. regularly visited pornographic websites, 20 percent of men and 13 percent of women while on the job.[10]

Using Internet pornography damages men in multiple ways. They suffer the guilt of doing something they know is wrong, and they endure the fear of being caught. We've seen that men engaged in pornography struggle more frequently with feelings of anger, bitterness, and hopelessness. Other studies document a link between pornography use and loneliness, as well as addiction to pornography and sexual dysfunction. From a spiritual perspective, the damage is even greater. The more a man is involved with pornography, the more he feels spiritually stalled, that he has to hide from others, and that he can't please God. Some theologians maintain that involvement in pornography can completely immobilize a man spiritually.

The ripple effects of men's struggle with porn have devastating effects on the women and children who love them. As licensed MFT and noted researcher Jill Manning points out, use of pornography is "incompatible with the characteristics of stable, healthy marriages."[11] Porn consumption leads to more separation and divorce,[12] a feeling of objectification by female partners,[13] decreased sexual intimacy among spouses,[14] increased emotional distance,[15] and increased likelihood of real-life extramarital affairs later on.[16]

The unavoidable conclusion: The temptation of Internet pornography poses a huge and dangerous threat to men and their families. Ministries like XXXChurch and New Life's *Every Man's Battle* are working to help those dealing with the guilt, shame, and pain of porn addiction. The problem is so widespread, and again, the lure is so nearly universal, that we desperately need to empower each man to fight the sexual temptations he faces each day.

Toward the end of the book, we'll look at practical and effective strategies for triumphing over temptations, including lust. If this is an area of struggle for you, please know you are not alone. There *is* hope, and this is a battle you *can* win. For now, acknowledging that the temptation is real and consuming is the first step in confronting and defeating it head on.

Hot Button #2: The Heart-Damaging Inflammation of Anger

While lust dominates as the most frequent male temptation, it's by no means the only one. Anger also figures prominently among what trips up men. Further, as these responses illustrate, the anger's source varies:

- "Being angry with my wife, losing my temper."
- "Becoming angry with my children or other people, or because of my circumstances."
- "Getting angry at God, not trusting Him, thinking He's no use to me, and wondering why He keeps proving it."
- "Being angry with others who have wronged me, and being hesitant to forgive them."
- "I want to slap most of our politicians and judges upside their heads."

Mosby's Medical Dictionary defines anger as "an emotional reaction characterized by extreme displeasure, rage, indignation, or hostility." This is a human response to feeling threatened or hurt in some way.

Anger seems to inundate us. Think back over the comments you've heard or online status updates you've read over the past week—how many were angry? Google "things that make me angry" and you'll get more than 182 million results,[17] including an untold number of "rant sites" specifically devoted to expressing anger.

What God Says About Anger

Stop being angry!

Turn from your rage!

Do not lose your temper—it only leads to harm.[18]

A gentle answer deflects anger, but harsh words make tempers flare.[19]

Be quick to listen, slow to speak, and slow to get angry. Human anger does not produce the righteousness God desires.[20]

Many of us seem under the impression that we have a right to express anger about anything, anytime. Why is that? Think about the other "deadly sins"—aren't we prone to try to conceal or deny them rather than publicize them? What is it about anger and *sharing* anger that's so alluring?

Physiologically, anger produces the "fight or flight" response, flooding your body with adrenaline and raising your heart rate. For most of us, this is unpleasant and detrimental, raising our risks for heart disease and heart attack. The body responds to anger as if under attack, releasing cholesterol and other chemicals that speed development of fatty deposits in the heart and the carotid arteries.

Repeated angry flare-ups—expressed *or* suppressed—have adverse long-term effects. For example, in a Johns Hopkins University study,[21] researchers followed almost two thousand medical students for more than thirty-six years. They found that those who angered easily were three times more likely to develop heart disease and five times more likely to suffer a heart attack.

Anger also takes a spiritual toll, supplanting the love and forgiveness for others that Jesus modeled and expects to foster in each of us. Biblically, God distinguishes between anger that results from the desires of our sinful flesh and anger that's a manifestation of

His righteousness, the latter resulting from witnessing offenses against God. It's not explosive, and it's slowly provoked.

When our participants talked about anger, though, the object of the anger was rarely an affront to God's righteousness. Most often the actions and words of other people are the source of our anger, and they offend us not because they violate God's holiness but because we perceive that in some way they threaten our own comfort, welfare, or happiness.

One strategy, then, for when we're tempted to be angry, is to stop and seek to consider the situation "through God's eyes." Is the root of our anger a real offense or is it based solely or primarily on our own vantage point? Many times this shift of perspective alone can dissipate a rising fury as we turn from our selfish desires and wants and look to our Father in heaven.

Also, we must have a strategy for how we'll respond in situations that make our blood boil. There's no upside to lashing out at or cold-shouldering the offender. God directs us to respond with wisdom, love, and gentleness.

Hot Button #3: Wringing (Instead of Raising) Our Hands

As an exercise, Pam made a list of things she's afraid of. Take a look, and then read her observations below:

(1) Deep water (think: the original *Jaws* movie)
(2) That dream with the faceless guy on the bed
(3) Being a complete failure/utter loser
(4) My husband dying

The list does go on; I (Pam) made it to test the love-is-the-opposite-of fear approach.[22] I do think that what I fear says a lot about where my heart actually is. If you break down my semi-sarcastic catalog of items, you'll find someone who's afraid of the unknown, is terrified of things larger than herself, has sexual insecurities, has always deep down felt insufficient, and fears losing everyone she loves. So where do I go with all that?

Even a cursory glance through the headlines has the potential to stir up worries about everything from finances to relationships to homeland security. It's no surprise that two of five people say they worry every day. Not surprising, but even so, it doesn't have to be that way.

Pam is right. As with most things, worry can have both a positive and a negative side to it. When, for example, our concerns focus on circumstances within our control and prompt us to take action to prevent something bad happening, worry can lead to productivity. Most of the time, though, we waste our energy worrying about things that are entirely out of our control or even our influence.

Just as with anger, anxiety can trigger our fight-or-flight response. Chronic worry damages our body. Studies have linked it with suppression of the immune system, digestive disorders, muscle tension, short-term memory loss, premature coronary artery disease, and heart attacks.

And consider this: 85 percent of the things we worry about *never happen.*[23] In addition, worrying about what might be supplants our trust in God. In essence, it moves us further from, instead of closer to, Jesus.

Gaining victory over the temptation to worry requires concerted daily effort. Connecting with God through prayer and His Word presents an opportunity to reflect again and again on His faithful, loving character and His promises to always care for you. It's also an opportunity to share with Him what's on your heart. He wants to hear it all because He loves you so much.

Don't let this connection end as you go about the rest of your daily life. Train yourself to recognize when worry is creeping in once more. Rather than giving in to it, redefine it as a "spiritual interruption." This is a perfect time to return again to the Word and to prayer, a time to reconnect and replace toxic worry with the life-giving promises of your Father.

What God Promises

Nothing is impossible with God.[24]

God has not given us a spirit of fear and timidity, but of power, love, and self-discipline.[25]

The floods have risen up, O Lord.

The floods have roared like thunder;

the floods have lifted their pounding waves.

But mightier than the violent raging of the seas,

mightier than the breakers on the shore—

the Lord above is mightier than these![26]

NUDGE FOUR: Change Your Brain

TEMPTED—Identifying Soul-Robbing Traps

I sometimes fall victim to wrong thinking and the Enemy's lies, including:

_____

_____

Of the "hot buttons" listed in this chapter, the one I'm most vulnerable to is:

_____

_____

I'd like Jesus to help me with:

_____

_____

_____

_____

_____

TESTED—Learning How to Break Free

What Research Confirms About "Training Our Brains" to Withstand Temptation:

Here's a growing trend among American believers: (1) We rationalize our behavior, (2) we ignore what the Bible says about sin, and (3) we haven't learned what it teaches about real transformation. We clean up after sin's messes, and we tell God we're sorry for our *foul-ups, goofs, blunders, mistakes, errors in judgment, flaws, weaknesses, shortcomings*—we use just about any word but *sin*. And then we go on living. But are we truly alive after we've entangled our lives with something so deadly?

A Proven Path:

(1) Change your attitude about sin.
(2) Change how your brain responds to temptation.

Many we've surveyed mention these keys to combating temptation:

- *Connection*—Through prayer and engaging the Bible, spend time with Jesus each day, or even better, several times a day.
- *Alertness*—Be aware of situations when you're likely to be tempted.
- *Scheme*—Set yourself up to avoid temptation. For example, if Internet porn tempts you, set your open Bible next to you while you're online.
- *Time-out*—When you feel the first tingle of temptation, stop. Take a deep breath. Reflect on what God would have you do in the situation.

What Christ-Followers Are Telling Us:

For most of my life I've felt like a spiritual mess—rarely close to Jesus, hardly ever understanding the Bible, and almost never withstanding temptation. I'd often ask myself, "How can Christianity really make a difference for me?" But then a Christian friend showed me that—even though I had committed my heart to Jesus—my mind was still tuned in to worldly ways of thinking—destructive thoughts, negativity, self-centeredness. He challenged me to be transformed and renewed daily by engaging, not merely reading, God's Word. It really works!

For the past year I've been on a quest to get closer to God, striving to live as Jesus did. I know that I'll never be able to follow the exact steps Christ took, which was to live a perfect life, but I can always try. I pray and read the Bible. I'm also connected to a community of believers. Here's what I'm discovering: Certain sins that used to weigh me down are becoming easier to withstand.

For the longest time, I rarely sensed God in my life. When I prayed, I felt as if I was merely talking to myself. My pastor gave me a bunch of happy talk and pat answers. He also gave me some Bible verses to read. (To be honest, I think he cares more about packing folks in on Sunday mornings and putting on glitzy programs than he does about connecting with real people with real problems.) Another friend handed me your other book, *Unstuck: Your Life. God's Design. Real Change.* He invited me to a small group that was studying it. Suddenly, it clicked. My thinking was all wrong. I was stuck in a worldly mindset—caught up in religion instead of relationship. And for most of my life I was reading the Bible instead of engaging it. Now I slow down, savor each word—filling my mind with truth and seeking connection with God.

TRUE—Charting a Path Toward Change

1. *RECEIVE God's Word.* Read or listen to Romans 12:1–8.
2. *REFLECT on verse 2.* Pull it apart word by word, seeking God's personal message to you. Invite His Spirit to speak.

Do not conform to the pattern of this world, but be transformed by the renewing of your mind. Then you will be able to test and approve what God's will is—his good, pleasing and perfect will.

What is God saying to you? After a moment of silence before Him, converse with Him (talk and listen) through prayer.
Begin with general thoughts and impressions . . .

- "Heavenly Father, here's what I feel when I read these verses":

- "Here's what's hard for me, God—what I don't understand":

Now relate these verses to your specific struggles:

- "Here's what Romans 12:1–8 is telling me about the wrong thinking that has infected my mind":

- "With your help, Lord, here's how I'll endeavor to give up the pattern of this world and allow you to renew my mind":

3. *MEMORIZE Romans 12:1.* Repeat it to yourself as often as needed. Write it out on an index card and post it where you'll see it.

"I urge you, brothers and sisters, in view of God's mercy, to offer your bodies as a living sacrifice, holy and pleasing to God—this is your true and proper worship."

4. LISTEN to a friend. James Emery White says, of sin's effects:

> Continued exposure to a sin such as pornography is like shooting
> Novocain into your soul. It deadens you and grieves the Holy Spirit
> in your life, forcing Him to withdraw His utmost filling in a way
> that diminishes His power and presence in your life.[27]

5. RESPOND to God's nudges. Try this brain-change exercise:

- As you study the chart below, consider two things about
  yourself: (1) the traps you've fallen into, and (2) how the
  truth can set you free.[28] Write down your thoughts in the
  appropriate boxes.

Soul-Robbing Trap	Wrong Thinking	Consequent Struggle	Right Thinking	Healing Path
Seeking Fulfillment From Successful Performance	Failure is completely unacceptable; I must measure up by attaining successful goals; I must perform well to be worthy.	Fear of failure; a compulsion to succeed; chronic perfectionism; driven incessantly toward attaining goals.	God has forgiven me through Christ. I am completely pleasing to Him. (Romans 3:24; 5:1–2; 2 Corinthians 5:19)	I am valuable just as I am. I do not have to perform or live up to impossible standards.
Basing Self-Worth on the Approval of Others	The approval of others makes me worthy.	Fear of rejection; people-pleasing; defensiveness; oversensitivity to criticism.	God has brought me back into relationship with Him through Christ. He fully accepts me. (Romans 5:8–10; 2 Corinthians 5:18–20; Colossians 1:21–22)	My self-worth isn't based on anyone else's opinion of me. I'm accepted just as I am.

Soul-Robbing Trap	Wrong Thinking	Consequent Struggle	Right Thinking	Healing Path
Condemning Ourselves (and Others) If We Fail	I am unworthy of love if I fail. When I do, I deserve condemnation and punishment.	Fear of punishment; prone to blame others for personal failures; driven to avoid failure.	God's wrath was satisfied through Christ's death on the cross. He loves and accepts me. (1 John 4:9–11; Jude 24)	I am not condemned, even if I fail. I'm loved just as I am.
Allowing Shame to De-motivate Our Desires	I am hopeless and unworthy; there is nothing acceptable about me. I am too far gone to change.	Fear of never being good enough for God; toxic sense of shame, inferiority.	God has given me new life through Christ. My character is changing radically from self-centeredness to God-centeredness. (Titus 3:5)	I am a new creation in Christ. I can start fresh every day of my life.

Performance Trap:

_____

_____

My Healing Path:

_____

_____

Approval Trap:

_____

_____

My Healing Path:

Blame Trap:

My Healing Path:

Shame Trap:

My Healing Path:

• Read the following excerpt (from *Change Your Brain, Change Your Life*), then answer the question below:

Thoughts are very powerful. They can make your mind and body feel good or they can make you feel bad. Every cell in your body is affected by every thought you have. That is why when people get emotionally upset they frequently develop physical symptoms, such as a headache or a stomachache. Some physicians think that people who have a lot of negative thoughts are more likely to get cancer. If you can think about good things, you will feel better. . . . You can train your thoughts to be positive and hopeful, or you can allow them to be negative and upset you. . . . One way to learn how to change your thoughts is to notice them when they are negative and talk back to them. When you just think a negative thought without challenging it, your mind believes it and your body reacts to it. When you correct negative thoughts, you take away their power over you.[29]

How can *I* overcome soul-robbing choices by changing my brain—by replacing lies, temptations, and negative thoughts with the truth?

_____

_____

_____

_____

6. *PRAY.* Consider expressing this prayer by Malcolm Muggeridge:

O God, stay with me; let no word cross my lips that is not your word, no thoughts enter my mind that are not your thoughts, no deed ever be done or entertained by me that is not your deed.[30]

5

Women at the Cross

Our Research Reveals Struggles Women Face

Fear is a struggle for me—not feeling good enough, pretty enough, or skinny enough to hold on to my husband. I am afraid of his leaving me for someone else even though we've been together for seventeen years. I feel like he is waiting for the better thing to come along, and then he will leave me. Along with that comes insecurity and jealousy, and then I turn to bulimia to help me lose weight so I won't lose him.

—Andrea

The desire to be beautiful has led to jealousy and controlling behaviors and some unfaithful thoughts toward someone who does seem to notice and desire me.

—Susan

My biggest temptation is to give up when relationships get hard. Some days it's not an issue.
Other days I have to ask God to just get me
through the day. My husband, who's supposed
to be a Christian, doesn't always look like he is,
with his attitudes and responses.

—Rebecca

I am unhealthy, and I feel Satan is pleased to keep
me preoccupied with this struggle in which I continually fail. At this point in my walk I'm not sure
if the temptation to overindulge in toxic foods is
my biggest challenge or if it's the temptation to
take my eyes off Jesus and spend too much time
and energy feeling guilty and defeated about my
poor health.

—Angela

Impatience and anger are big issues for me. My
mother, who is ninety, lives with us. I sometimes get
impatient with how slow her responses are, though
I try to keep those feelings from her. I get angry
with my husband too. He can be very domineering.

—Sara

Men don't have a corner on the "temptation/sin marketplace."
As you'll hear us repeat in so many words throughout this book,
We all struggle with something. While women, on average, may
encounter fewer temptations than men in a given day, most women,
on most days, feel tempted in some way. Believe me I (Pam) know
this from firsthand experience.

Note: Pam is talking here.

When we ask women our open-ended question about what tempts them, things get messy and personal. Instead of one predominant theme, several common and very personal areas of struggle emerge. Amid the diversity of issues, most frequently there's anger at others (often husbands), gossip, worry, overeating, and poor use of time and money.

For women, most temptations seem to occur in the context of relationships. Consider these descriptions women gave:

- "To tell off my manager and quit my job. To get rid of the dog and tell my son he ran away."
- "Letting my anger get the best of me; yelling and belittling my spouse or kids."

- "Talking about others at work, being unkind when I think they're abusing the workplace."
- "Gossiping about an injustice to my husband by his son. Worrying about the possibility of that gossip coming back to haunt me."
- "I'm separated from my husband and have sometimes been tempted to try to make myself more attractive to a male counselor that I know."

Let's take a closer look at five of the "hot buttons" for women, the temptations with which women most often struggle.

Hot Button #1: Fretting About Families, Friends, and Frames

That the birds of worry and
care fly over your head, this you cannot
change, but that they build nests in
your hair, this you can prevent.[1]

Worry is by far the most common enticement for women. Three of five call it a top temptation and/or confront fear or anxiety at least once a week.

Many fears and worries focus on loved ones—family and friends. It's no coincidence that in the U.S., as well as in many other nations, women remain the primary caregivers of children, the sick, the disabled, and the elderly.

How should we respond when worries about those we love invade our minds? Some of the tips shared earlier bear repeating here. First, remember that the vast majority of what we worry about never comes to pass. Next, take time to connect with your heavenly

---

ON WOMEN AND CAREGIVING

The role of caregiver is a broad one, encompassing nurturer, cheerleader, health provider, teacher, care manager, companion, surrogate decision-maker, and advocate. Being so intimately involved in others' physical, emotional, and spiritual well-being, it's only natural to be concerned about them as well. Concern can become a problem when it turns to worry, which supplants our faith and trust in God by doubting or denying that He loves our loved ones even more than we do and will care for them.

Father through prayer and His Word. Reflect on His loving and faithful character and the promises contained in His love letter to you. As your day progresses, remain alert to worry creeping in, and use those times as opportunities to return again to the cross.

Body image is another common realm of worry. For one thing, for most women there's a big disconnect between media portrayals of feminine beauty and what they see in their own mirrors. The average American woman is 5'4" and weighs 140 to150 pounds; the average American fashion model is 5'11" and weighs 117 pounds (an unhealthy weight for her height). Given our culture's emphasis on physical beauty—not to mention its shifting determinations of what "beauty" is—we shouldn't be surprised that most teen girls say they're unhappy with their bodies and that 40 to 50 percent of women are trying to lose weight at any point in time.

Worry alone causes physical damage, as explained in chapter 4. When worry focuses on body image, it can have additional devastating effects. According to the National Eating Disorder Association, an estimated ten million American women suffer from eating disorders. Anorexia and bulimia have the highest mortality rates of all mental illnesses—20 percent of sufferers without treatment die from their infirmity.

When women worry that they aren't "good enough," their relationships are often impacted as well. Jealousy, envy, and anxiety, or panic about being rejected or abandoned, can become all-consuming. Worry may lead to self-disparaging remarks about yourself, which are deeply painful for those who love you most. No one wants to hear the apple of his eye maligned.

This last point also relates to how worry about ourselves can affect our relationship with God. The One who loves us more than we can imagine hears what we say to ourselves—that we're not pretty enough, thin enough, smart enough. . . . Just as we're hurt when our children disparage themselves, our negative statements about ourselves wound our heavenly Father.

How should we deal with the temptation to worry? In short, we must keep temptation from building a nest in our minds by changing what we reflect on and believe. Instead of comparing ourselves to fashion models or celebrities, or anyone else, we are to ponder and embrace what *God* says about us:

- He formed you . . . wonderfully![2]
- He sees the beauty of your inner self, a gentle and quiet spirit.[3]
- He loves you so much He gave His Son for you.[4]
- He delights in you and rejoices over you with singing.[5]
- You are His treasured possession.[6]

Hot Button #2: Letting Anger's Flame Ignite Unkind Thoughts

In our research, anger emerged as the second most common issue for women. More than one-third listed it as a top temptation, again, most often in the context of relationships. Many spoke of anger toward their spouse—from frustration over daily disagreements to lingering pain and bitterness from past hurts. Others talked of feeling anger toward parents and children.

Anger toward God also is common. In a series of studies by Dr. Julie Exline, 60 percent of adults described some level of anger at God. Painful incidents like bereavement, illness, accidents, and relationship problems were the most frequent reasons.[7] Annette described such an experience:

> A couple years ago I was very angry that something I loved was taken away from me. It was something that started as a thing for God but slowly became less and less of God and more and more secular. I had that feeling in the pit of my stomach that being part of it had become wrong, so I cut myself off from it, trying to do what I know God was telling me to do. But then I resented God for taking this wonderful, fulfilling thing out of my life. I couldn't understand why He took it from me. It impacted my life for probably over a year.

We discussed in chapter 4 how the body's reaction to feeling angry damages the heart. Often seen as a "men's problem," more women than men die from heart disease each year. Today heart disease is the leading cause of death among American women, accounting for one-third of all deaths.

DEALING WITH ANGER: TENDENCIES

While men and women have similar rates of experiencing anger, they usually deal with it differently. Psychologists like Dr. Raymond DiGiuseppe of St. John's University have found that men express anger more often through aggression or through impulsive actions. Due in part to differences in how they're raised, women more often turn to gossip, to "writing off" the offender, or to trying to talk about and resolve the problem. Perhaps because they're less likely to express anger, women tend to be angry longer, more resentful, and they report more difficulty with forgiving those who have hurt them.

It's worth repeating too that anger takes a *spiritual* toll. For women especially, holding on to anger can block us from loving and forgiving others as Jesus would. Learning to identify what triggers anger, sharing concerns with God through prayer, and reflecting on what His Word says about the issue can help avoid the temptation of anger. It will go a long way toward minimizing the heart damage—physical and spiritual—that is caused by anger.

Hot Button #3: Getting Consumed by Thoughts of Consuming

[Eve] saw that the tree was beautiful and its fruit looked delicious, and she wanted the wisdom it would give her. So she took some of the fruit and ate it.[8]

The two biggest sellers in bookstores are the cookbooks and the diet books. The cookbooks tell you how to prepare the food and the diet books tell you how not to eat any of it.[9]

God designed our bodies to require regular intake of nutrients for energy and health. Voltaire mused, long ago, that "nothing would be more tiresome than eating and drinking, if God had not made them a pleasure as well as a necessity." But many of us have a complex relationship with food.

We live in a society that places untenable emphasis on physical beauty and on thinness as a central feature of that beauty. Most of us carry more pounds around with us than we're told (and shown) that we should.

Our relationship with food also plays a significant role in our overall health. News reports regularly remind us that our nation faces a serious health crisis, with one-third of adults and 17 percent of children being obese. Obesity raises risks for several serious health problems, such as diabetes, joint pain and damage, and heart disease. According to one study, the medical costs of obesity topped $147 billion domestically in 2008.

Given the societal messages that "thin is better" and the warnings about the health dangers of being overweight, it's not surprising that so many women—about three out of ten in our studies—see food as a temptation. A vast library of Christian diet books likewise encourages Christ-followers to slim down through prayer and devotionals and sometimes traditional calorie-counting and exercise. Sales of spiritually focused diet books remain strong, indicating that myriads of dieters are seeking God's help in what they see as their battle with food and weight.

However, what really *is* the spiritual issue with food and weight? Our culture celebrates both thinness *and* indulgence, thus we must peel back the layers of our assumptions and presuppositions. R. Marie Griffith observes:

> What marks the more recent literature as distinctive is not its concern with corporeal thinness and good health per se but the apparent willingness of authors to accept, ardently and without flinching, the somatic standards of the wider culture and convert them into divine decree.
>
> Here and elsewhere, diet writers display too little critical reflection on the profaner sources of these assumptions. . . . The message of the Christian diet and fitness industry may still work to perpetuate the most harmful stereotypes of those in our society who are heavier than the latest faddish norm, reinforcing the double jeopardy of being a "fat" Christian in America. Often enough it slides alarmingly close to depicting a God who loves a size six woman more than a size sixteen.[10]

The critical question when we consider food as a temptation is whether in God's eyes it is in fact a temptation. In other words, are our notions about whether eating (or not eating) a certain amount or consuming (or not consuming) certain types of foods in line with His Word? We need biblical answers about food and eating. God tells us:

- We're not to worry about what we'll eat.[11]
- We're not to seek after food, to live with the goal of filling our bellies and titillating our taste buds.[12]
- We're to give thanks and be content in all circumstances.[13]

That's more than straightforward. But . . . what about answers to our more specific questions? For instance, how *much* does God want us to eat? Are certain types of food more pleasing to Him? Did He feel anger (or something else) when I ate that second brownie before bed last night?

The truth is that when we study His Word, we find that God doesn't emphasize these things. Therefore, neither should we. We're to be concerned about our relationship with food and our bodies only to the extent that it affects our ability to serve Jesus. As Steve Lehrer said:

> In order for us to understand what Scripture says about eating, we need to grasp the fact that *God wants us to be a people who are consumed with loving and serving Christ who also just happen to eat food*, rather than a people who are consumed with food, our bodies, and stimulating our taste buds who also just happen to be Christians. In light of this, we need to develop eating habits (or ways of thinking about eating) that make us more effective servants of Christ and we need to discontinue any eating habits (or ways of thinking about eating) that hinder us from being effective servants of Christ.[14]

How then should women of faith deal with situations where they feel food is a temptation? Begin by reflecting on how what

God does and does not say about eating relates to your life. Ask yourself whether you're feeling tempted to go against His will or if the feeling of temptation comes from another source, say, your desire to be a certain size. Share your struggles with your Father in heaven. Let Him renew your mind and your heart in this area.

Hot Button #4: Conveying Stolen Goods With Words

> *"Listening to gossip can be likened to receiving stolen goods; it puts you in immediate collusion with the person conveying the gossip to you. . . . The most enticing gossip is that which is highly feasible, often uncheckable, and deeply damning of the person who is its subject."*[15]

As I (Arnie) write, a smattering of headlines about various celebrities seductively shouts from the Yahoo! main page. One talks of a certain nonagenarian, father of a famous actor and producer, who's filing for divorce. Reading such news can set the wheels of my mind spinning with all sorts of comments and questions . . . when, truth be told, it's absolutely none of my business.

We're back at the matter of gossip. More than a quarter of the women we've surveyed said it's a common personal temptation. Many also recognize the damage and destruction gossip can bring:

Gossip has gotten me into trouble even when I've just shared with my husband. He gets upset and tells others . . . and it comes back to me eventually. Also, gossip by others has led to lies being told about my husband and me.

—Megan

Gossip. It never starts out that way, but I know in my heart it's wrong. I think I'm being "concerned" when in fact it's gossip any way you look at it.

—Keira

Women are twice as likely as men to feel tempted by gossip. Differences in topics to which men and women typically gravitate may partially explain why. Linguistic studies reveal that men's conversations most commonly focus on sports, careers, leisure activities, and politics; women more often discuss feelings, motivations, relationships, and personal problems. If we understand gossip as "rumor, or talk of a personal, sensational, or intimate nature,"[16] we can see how gossip could creep repeatedly into what began as appropriate conversation.

These can be hard words to take, especially for those of us who tend to justify our gossiping with the excuse that it's motivated out of concern for others and "was meant to lead to praying for them." The reality is, even if the motivation is thought to be compassion or concern, speculating about another person is wrong. It's far better to go directly to the person than risk marring or ruining their reputation. *Then* we can offer to pray for them.

A good place to start in dealing with the temptation to gossip is to spend time reflecting on what God says about it. Ask Him to speak to your heart and help you use your words to encourage others. When gossip is encroaching or approaching, do a quick "heart check." Is the conversation sticking with facts or in the realm of guesswork or hearsay? What's your motive for speaking, or listening?

WHAT GOD SAYS ABOUT GOSSIP

Conversations cross the line when they turn toward analysis of why certain events are occurring in the lives of a third party. Speculating about the intimate details of another's private life reveals a heart that is standing in a pose of judgment. Thus gossip is a spiritual problem. And God clearly shows us why it's wrong. Gossip is a hurtful[17] product of idleness[18] we're to avoid[19] and to halt by *not* passing it on.[20] The tongue's propensity to spread gossip *comes from hell itself*.[21] Consider the following contemporary imagery:

> Prior and current marriage trouble, children's problems, bad-boy boyfriends and control-freak girlfriends, affairs, unplanned pregnancies, diseases—it was like a swarm of flies going round and round over a group of leering, grinning faces at a carnival.[22]

> Gossip is *not* conversation. It is the spewing forth of audible venom that poisons and eventually kills not only those who hear it or are the subject of it but also those who choose to speak it. Those of us who choose to participate in it are hissing snakes coiled up and waiting for our prey to get within striking distance. Nothing good comes of it. It is not entertainment. It is not playful banter. It is evil spoken to and about another human being that destroys the very fabric of the breathtaking and beautiful tapestry that is human encounter.[23]

If what's being said was about you, and you weren't present, would you want it said? Finally, when you need to, use the power of silence to stop the conversation and let gossip go no further.

Hot Button #5: Letting "Disappointed" Become "Discouraged"

Throughout life we encounter disappointments. Some are momentary, like when the grocery store is out of your favorite brand of coffee. Others are more long-lasting . . . a wayward child, a chronic illness, a troubled marriage, financial calamity. At times, when we survey the situation, we feel our future can't possibly bring joy or pleasure, only more anguish and difficulty.

> **"Disappointments will come and go,**
> **but discouragement is a choice you make."**[24]

Such feelings of discouragement are a common temptation for both men and women. Among Christ-followers, almost half of women feel discouraged at least once a month. Temptation to give in to discouragement is a powerful weapon Satan uses to steal our vitality and hope. It's a lie that denies the truth: Jesus *is* our all-satisfying Treasure, and those who know Him have *today* the certain hope of beholding Him forever.[25]

Discouragement saps our energy and focus. It makes us want to do as Elijah did: sit under a solitary tree and pray for the Lord to take us home.[26]

How do we avoid this trap? The first and most important step is to turn to Jesus just as you are—even if you're thirsty,[27] heavy-laden and fatigued,[28] and weak in faith.[29] *Don't wait!* Spend some time reminding yourself of the eternal hope that is yours through Christ. Also remember that no matter how strong they feel emotions are temporary and don't always reflect reality.

Words to Renew Your Spirit

Do take time to care for yourself. Temptation's lure is strongest when we're worn out. Elijah is a prime example; he struggled with discouragement after defeating the prophets of Baal.[30] The restoration of his physical strength through rest and nourishment was a key part of regaining his hope.

As you feel your hope and joy in Him return, ask the Lord to work in your situation. If possible, find another Christ-follower and let her pray for you. Disappointments will come, but falling prey to discouragement is a decision. Through your relationship with Jesus, you have all you need to choose hope instead.

NUDGE FIVE: Interrupt Your Heart

TEMPTED—Identifying Soul-Robbing Traps

On many days, my mind often is bogged down by these struggles:

Here's how my preoccupation with daily troubles interferes with God's voice:

I'd like Jesus to help me with:

TESTED—Learning How to Break Free

What Research Confirms About "Spiritual Interruptions":

There are times during a twenty-four-hour cycle when we're most susceptible to temptation. It's different for every person, and it's based upon a variety of factors: the types of temptations a person deals with, spiritual maturity, family/church support, degree of stress encountered daily, emotions, physical condition, etc.

During our most vulnerable moments, we can be strengthened by a scriptural touch. We call this a "spiritual interruption," and you can receive them in a variety of ways—through a smartphone (which we recommend if you have access), an MP3 player, software, email, or the tried-and-true method of cracking open your Bible. For more on this, read the "Respond" section below and go to www.tempted.gotandem.com.

A Proven Path:

(1) Interrupt your thoughts with Scripture four or more times a day.

(2) Hide God's Word in your heart.

God's Word hidden in our hearts fortifies us against temptation's power. But there's much more to it than memorizing verses. Receiving multiple "interruptions" throughout the day makes the difference.

What Christ-Followers Are Telling Us:

My life has changed radically ever since I started doing three things: (1) engaging the Bible daily, not just reading it, (2) finding meaningful connections with other believers through church and small groups, and (3) allowing my heart to be spiritually interrupted throughout the day. These really work.

I struggle with pride, and my stubborn will and insensitive tongue often get me into trouble. I think pride is one of the worst temptations—the source of so many others. Instead of just reading a passage from the Bible in the morning, I receive Scripture through texts and emails all throughout the day. It really helps me to guard my tongue and keep my heart focused on what God wants.

TRUE—Charting a Path Toward Change

1. *RECEIVE God's Word.* Read or listen to Psalm 119:1–16.
2. *REFLECT on verses 10–12.* Pull them apart sentence by sentence, seeking God's personal message to you. Invite His Spirit to speak.

> I seek you with all my heart;
>> do not let me stray from your commands.
> I have hidden your word in my heart
>> that I might not sin against you.
> Praise be to you, LORD;
>> teach me your decrees.

What is God saying to you? After a moment of silence before Him, converse with Him (talk and listen) through prayer.

Begin with general thoughts and impressions . . .

- "Heavenly Father, here's what I feel when I read these verses":

- "Here's what's hard for me, God—what I don't understand":

Now relate these verses to your specific struggles:

- "Here's what Psalm 119:1–16 is telling me about the power of your Word":

- "With your help, Lord, here's how I'll endeavor to hide your Word in my heart in order to withstand temptation":

3. *MEMORIZE Psalm 119:1–2.* Repeat it to yourself as often as needed. Write it out on an index card and post it where you'll see it.

> Blessed are those whose ways are blameless,
>   who walk according to the law of the LORD.
> Blessed are those who keep his statutes
>   and seek him with all their heart.

4. *LISTEN to a friend.* Marjorie Thompson says, of God's steady gaze:

> While the truth that we cannot escape God's all-seeing eye may weigh us down at times, it is finally the only remedy for our uneasiness. If we wish to hide from the penetrating gaze of holy love, it is because we know it falls on what is unholy and unloving within us. Only under God's steady gaze of love are we able to find the healing and restoration we so desperately need.[31]

5. *RESPOND to God's nudges.* Try this spiritual-interruption exercise:

- Refer to "My Spiritual Weakness Chart" (chapter 2 [see "Respond"] and Worksheet 1 [at end of book]). What weaknesses did you uncover during a seven-day period? What temptations did they lead to? What kinds of issues did you log on your worksheet?

- Using Mike as an example: He identified stress, which for him often leads to the temptations of fear, worry, and anxiety . . . leaving him prey to sins like anger and sloth. Mike entered that information into his chart. Next, he determined when he needed to be spiritually interrupted during a twenty-four-hour cycle—those moments when he needed to *get his mind off his struggle* and *get his heart focused on God*. He transferred key observations to the "My Spiritual Interruptions Chart" (see sample below). We've provided a blank chart for you to fill in (see Worksheet 2: My Spiritual Interruptions Chart at end of book).

- He subscribed to our ministry's spiritual-growth services (goTandem.com). He signed up for daily scriptural touches about his needs, delivered at the times when he's most likely to feel tempted.

- Consider logging on to www.tempted.gotandem.com. You'll find a detailed explanation of the interruptions you can receive from us!

MY SPIRITUAL INTERRUPTIONS CHART
How Mike's Heart Is "Interrupted" Throughout the Day

24-Hour Cycle	When Temptation Is Strongest	How I Feel	Specific Struggle	Spiritual Interruption
Late Night: 12:00–3:00	*Often have trouble shutting off brain, going to sleep*	*Worried and anxious*	*Worry/Fear*	*Recite key memorization verse (e.g., Romans 8:31–32) before bed*
Earliest Morning: 3:00–6:00				

24-Hour Cycle	When Temptation Is Strongest	How I Feel	Specific Struggle	Spiritual Interruption
Early Morning (Day): 6:00–9:00	*As I think on stressful situations I'll face during the day*	*Slight-to-moderate worry and anxiety*	*Worry/Fear*	*Email from goTandem. com worry track*
Midmorning: 9:00–12:00	*As I tackle workload*	*Slight-to-moderate worry and anxiety*	*Worry/Fear*	*Voice message with Scripture (from goTandem)*
Noon Hour: 12:00–1:00				
Early Afternoon: 1:00–2:00				
Midafternoon: 3:00–5:00				
Early Evening: 5:00–7:00	*As I wrap up workday*	*Slight-to-moderate worry and anxiety*	*Worry/Fear*	*Text message with Scripture (from goTandem)*
Midevening: 7:00–9:00				
Late Evening: 9:00–12:00				

- Try this approach to fighting temptation for at least forty days, and then jot down what you've observed about your spiritual life:

My struggles with temptation:

_____

_____

My relationship with God:

_____

_____

My relationship with friends and family:

_____

_____

How I feel about myself:

_____

_____

6. PRAY. Consider expressing this prayer by Thomas à Kempis:[32]

> *In confidence of your goodness and great mercy, O Lord, I draw near to you, as a sick person to the Healer, as one hungry and thirsty to the Fountain of Life, a creature to the Creator, a desolate soul to my own tender Comforter. Behold, in you is everything that I can or ought to desire. You are my salvation and my redemption, my Helper and my strength.*

6

Kelly's Story:
Addiction and Grace

When Alcohol Robs a Family

Imagine being seven years old and begging your mother to stop drinking.

"Just stop . . . please, Mommy, stop doing that. And wake up." You tug on her sleeve and try to nudge her out of bed—nudge her into loving you . . . to somehow become more like other kids' parents.

"Okay, yes . . . yes, sweetie. Mommy promises." Slurred words stick to her tongue. "I'll stop. Mommy isn't feeling well, so give me a few minutes to get up—"

But soon she'd latch on to another bottle. She'd step right back into the ugly cycle of broken promises and yet another drink. As the saying goes, "One drink is one too many—but a thousand is not enough." It simply never stops. It just keeps happening . . . over and over and over.

My name is Kelly. That's how it was for me. That was my childhood. I felt scared and alone. I desperately needed my mom, yet alcohol was robbing our family—stealing the intimate connection every child needs with a parent, violating trust. All I could do was watch as her addiction slowly dragged her right out of my life.

Here's the thing: My mom wasn't only an alcoholic, she was also mentally ill. Her severe depression made her suicidal, and she'd often try to kill herself.

When my siblings or I would find her unconscious, we'd have to figure out whether she was passed out from drinking or had overdosed again. If it was an overdose, we'd call my dad and he'd race home from work. I don't know why we never called 9-1-1. Maybe because we weren't supposed to tell anyone?

My dad would take Mom to the ER to have her stomach pumped, and they'd admit her to the psych ward. Then he'd bring home McDonald's for dinner and we'd all go on like normal, because that *was* our normal.

We weren't allowed to tell the secret of my mom's alcoholism and mental illness, so a sense of shame settled over our family. I remember bursting out crying in fourth grade after my teacher innocently said, "Have your mom help you with your homework tonight." She didn't know my mom was in the mental hospital.

🍎 🍎 🍎

Fast-forward to my teen years . . .

One time when my mom was in the hospital, she wrote me a letter apologizing for an attempted suicide. She told me she was sorry, but that when she'd tried to talk to me about her problems I hadn't listened. I was thirteen then, only a middle-schooler. Yet my mom expected me to be able to process her issues and help her solve them when even a trained psychiatrist couldn't. This cemented the sense that her problems weren't mine.

🍎 🍎 🍎

Fast-forward to high school graduation . . .

My dad was scheduled to work a late shift that night, and my mom said she didn't feel well enough to attend. So I sat in my cap and gown, trying not to cry and wondering who would care when they called my name. I believed beyond a doubt that I had no worth and that no one did care about me.

Addiction Steals and Kills

In addition to my personal value and security, my childhood experiences robbed me of a sense of family. I spent the next few years making bad decisions, searching for someone to give me a sense of worth. Thankfully, in my late twenties, I entered a relationship with God.

As my friendship with Him grew, I initially tried to fix my relationship with my mother. My three siblings were estranged from her, but still I tried to maintain the relationship. God had said, "Honor your father and mother."

It's interesting that as children, my siblings and I never talked about the hurt and disappointment, the lack of care, or any detail of our upbringing. My parents' "Don't tell" message somehow filtered into our entire existence.

As adults we began to share more. When I told my sister a particularly painful story of finding my mom unconscious, she said, "I was there." We both remembered the event from our own point of view, but neither of us could recall the other's presence. The isolation and shame of our childhood literally stole from us the camaraderie of siblings. We were cheated out of a relationship with the only other people who could understand exactly what we were going through.

I sought counseling—first in a group session with my mom. Afterward the counselor gave me valuable advice: "Guard your heart. Your mom is the most manipulative person I have ever met." This gave me permission to set boundaries with my mom. Eventually they would become permanent.

🍎 🍎 🍎

I married and had children. On a visit with my mom, my then-four-year-old daughter handed her a picture she'd colored. "Do you like it, Grandma?"

She answered, "It's okay; you could have done better." And I saw that flicker of pain in my daughter's eyes I recognized only too well. *Why is someone who's supposed to love and support me saying something so hurtful to me? Am I valuable? Am I loved?*

I had tried to keep the relationship alive. But I realized that if I wasn't strong enough to end it for myself, I had to end it for my child. The bond was toxic. I'd been robbed of my sense of worth, but I would protect my daughter.

There's a terrible void that comes from not having a loving mom. Even so, I continued to seek God as my parent. "As a mother comforts her child, so will I comfort you,"[1] He has pledged. He has promised to comfort—to protect, to shelter, to support, to uplift—like a loving mother would.

Grace Gives Back

Over time, God healed my wounds. Not only did He show me that He's my perfect parent, He also put loving women in my life when I needed them. Special teachers, precious friends, even my mother-in-law helped fill the void. I called these women my "manna moms." Just as God provided the Israelites enough bread, enough "manna" for each day,[2] so He provided me with enough mothering for each time I needed it.

Occasionally my mom would still call, seemingly only to wound me. On one message she said, "You are everything that's wrong with the Christian faith. I am embarrassed of you." Mad at myself, as much as at her—because I'd listened to the voicemail and not just deleted it as I should have—I stewed angrily and thought, *I hate her. I really hate her.*

I'd not allowed myself those words before, even though I'd felt I had grounds to do so. Finally I gave myself permission . . . but it did not make me feel better. It made me feel worse. And I felt like the devil smiled.

So I said out loud, "I forgive you, Mom." I felt a twinge in my heart. *What* was *that? Could it be joy?* I said it again, louder: "I forgive you, Mom."

Then I said it twice more. Then I started thanking and praising God that He forgives me. I was filled with such abundant joy.

Does this mean we all live happily ever after? No. I'm still estranged from my mom. But I can forgive her, even without her asking for it. I can be joyful despite the pain, and because of the forgiveness.

Living With Addiction . . . Responding With Grace

The devil comes to steal, and kill, and destroy.[3] He had stolen my childhood stability. He had killed my dreams of having a loving mom. He had destroyed my family. But he cannot destroy the person whom God would have me be, because while he steals, God restores. God did not restore the relationship with my mom, but He did restore my sense of security, worth, and peace.

In the past I've read stories of difficult relationships like mine. Often, it seems someone prays and eventually the relationship is healed. Those stories made me ask, again, "What is wrong with me? Are my prayers ineffective? Why doesn't God care about me?"

God does care about me. For one thing, my story of a relationship that stays broken may heal others in broken relationships. God chooses sometimes to heal us, not our relationships. And it doesn't mean He loves us any less.

I have a dream. When I go to heaven, I'll see my mom there. And we both will be perfected in Christ. We'll have no more pain or anger. No more mental illness or addiction. And finally we can have a relationship. But even if *that* doesn't happen, I will be okay. I already have the perfect Parent.

🍎　🍎　🍎

I've learned to look to Jesus' example in difficult relationships.

Jesus entered a house, and again a crowd gathered, so that he and his disciples were not even able to eat. When his family heard about this, they went to take charge of him, for they said, "He is out of his mind." . . .

Jesus' mother and brothers arrived. Standing outside, they sent someone in to call him. A crowd was sitting around him, and they told him, "Your mother and brothers are outside looking for you."

"Who are my mother and my brothers?" he asked.

Then he looked around at those seated in a circle around him and said, "Here are my mother and my brothers! Whoever does God's will is my brother and sister and mother."[4]

The *NIV Study Bible*[5] explains that Jesus' answer was not a rejection of His natural family but an affirmation of His higher priority on relationship to those who believed in Him—those who had joined His spiritual family.

I am estranged from my mom. My estrangement was not meant to reject her. It was a means of self-preservation; it was to keep from being destroyed by the pain of our relationship. All the godly women God has put in my life, the women who "believe in me," they are my mother.

To anyone who's ever had a difficult relationship with their own family: Follow Jesus' example. Don't reject them; embrace those around you. They are your mother, sister, brother. They believe in you.

If Addiction Robs Your Family

(1) Seek God to be your perfect parent. He can fill any gap left by poor parenting.

(2) Don't try to fix anyone else. You didn't cause their problem. You can't control it. You can't cure it.[6]

(3) Seek counseling to help heal the wounds of a broken relationship.

(4) Set healthy boundaries. Guard your heart. Refuse to speak with the person when they are drunk or volatile. You have permission to say no, not answer calls, and not listen to abusive messages.

(5) Forgive. It's not just a tip—it's a divine mandate. Forgiveness does not necessarily mean staying in relationship with that person.

(6) Surround yourself with loving, supportive people who believe in you.

Healing Bible Verses to Explore

Psalm 30:2: Lord my God, I called to you for help, and you healed me.

Psalm 41:3: The Lord sustains them on their sickbed and restores them from their bed of illness.

Psalm 147:3: He heals the brokenhearted and binds up their wounds.

Isaiah 53:5: He was pierced for our transgressions, he was crushed for our iniquities; the punishment that brought us peace was on him, and by his wounds we are healed.

Jeremiah 17:14: Heal me, Lord, and I will be healed; save me and I will be saved, for you are the one I praise.

Hosea 14:4: I will heal their waywardness and love them freely, for my anger has turned away from them.

Malachi 4:2: For you who revere my name, the sun of righteousness will rise with healing in its rays. And you will go out and frolic like well-fed calves.

Matthew 8:8: The centurion replied, "Lord, I do not deserve to have you come under my roof. But just say the word, and my servant will be healed."

Matthew 8:16: Many who were demon-possessed were brought to him, and he drove out the spirits with a word and healed all the sick.

Matthew 9:35: Jesus went through all the towns and villages, teaching in their synagogues, proclaiming the good news of the kingdom and healing every disease and sickness.

Matthew 19:2: Large crowds followed him, and he healed them there.

Mark 5:34: Daughter, your faith has healed you. Go in peace and be freed from your suffering.

Luke 8:50: Jesus said to Jairus, "Don't be afraid; just believe, and she will be healed."

Luke 9:11: He welcomed [the crowds] and spoke to them about the kingdom of God, and healed those who needed healing.

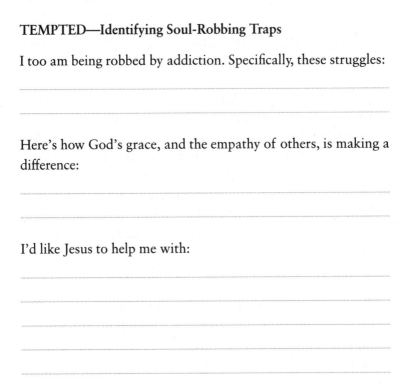

NUDGE SIX: "Detach" Attachments

TEMPTED—Identifying Soul-Robbing Traps

I too am being robbed by addiction. Specifically, these struggles:

Here's how God's grace, and the empathy of others, is making a difference:

I'd like Jesus to help me with:

TESTED—Learning How to Break Free

What Research Confirms About Addictive Processes:

Every day at goTandem—a division of Back to the Bible—our team of spiritual-growth encouragers makes thousands of calls to Christians worldwide. Their goal: Listen to what's on the hearts of believers, encourage them to persevere in their faith, and pray with them. And they hear the same agonized cries from people of all walks of life: "Pray for a family member who's battling an addiction"; "Pray for me—I'm simply clueless about how to overcome my struggle"; "Pray, please pray. My life is a mess."

Here's what we've learned: Far too many of us mistakenly believe that we are too far gone—that somehow God has given up on us and won't or can't forgive our sins. Isn't it time we break free from these lies?

Addiction expert Gerald G. May says, on the processes at work in us all:

> I am not being flippant when I say that all of us suffer from addiction, nor am I reducing the meaning of addiction. I mean in all truth that the psychological, neurological, and spiritual dynamics of full-fledged addiction are actively at work in every human being. The same processes that are responsible for addiction to alcohol and narcotics are also responsible for addiction to ideas, work, relationships, power, moods, fantasies, and an endless variety of other things. We are all addicts in every sense of the word.[7]

A Proven Path:

(1) Admit what's enslaving you—to yourself and to God.
(2) Find the counsel of a trusted friend.
(3) Be empowered by the Holy Spirit.

Dr. May goes on to say our addictions are our own worst enemies. They enslave us with chains of our own making and yet are beyond our control:

> Addiction also makes idolaters of us all because it forces us to worship these objects of attachment, thereby preventing us from truly, freely loving God and one another. . . . Yet, in still another paradox, our addictions can lead us to a deep appreciation of grace. They can bring us to our knees.[8]

What Christ-Followers Are Telling Us:

From my personal experience with enslaving addictions and sins, merely being told to "read more Scripture" or "go to church more" angers me. It's insensitive when Christ-followers say these things because it shows no understanding of a person's enslavement. A slave isn't always free to do these things. These steps are often foreign to them. Instead, they need a hug, a smile, a listening ear—a daily nudge away from their addiction. Change isn't even possible until an enslaved person reaches bottom, cries out to his or her Savior, and has consistent counsel and accountability.

Once I reached my breaking point and admitted my struggle, three steps have helped me break free, stay free, and heal: (1) empowerment by the Holy Spirit, (2) encouragement from a mentor, and (3) daily doses of God's Word.

TRUE—Charting a Path Toward Change

1. *RECEIVE God's Word.* Read or listen to Isaiah 58.
2. *REFLECT on verses 6–9.* Pull them apart phrase by phrase, seeking God's personal message to you. Invite His Spirit to speak.

Is not this the kind of fasting I have chosen:
to loose the chains of injustice
    and untie the cords of the yoke,
to set the oppressed free
    and break every yoke?
Is it not to share your food with the hungry
    and to provide the poor wanderer with shelter—
when you see the naked, to clothe them,
    and not to turn away from your own flesh and blood?
Then your light will break forth like the dawn,
    and your healing will quickly appear;
then your righteousness will go before you,
    and the glory of the LORD will be your rear guard.
Then you will call, and the LORD will answer;
    you will cry for help, and he will say: Here am I.

What is God saying to you? After a moment of silence before Him, converse with Him (talk and listen) through prayer.
Begin with general thoughts and impressions . . .

- "Heavenly Father, here's what I feel when I read these verses":

_____

_____

- "Here's what's hard for me, God—what I don't understand":

_____

_____

Now relate these verses to your specific struggles:

- "Here's what Isaiah 58 is telling me about your power, your mercy, your desire to 'loose the chains' in my life":

_____

_____

_____

- "With your help, Lord—no matter what—here's how I'll endeavor to trust you today, to take a new step in a new direction ":

_____

_____

3. **MEMORIZE Isaiah 58:11.** Repeat it to yourself as often as needed. Write it out on an index card and post it where you'll see it.

> The LORD will guide you always;
>   he will satisfy your needs in a sun-scorched land
>   and will strengthen your frame.
> You will be like a well-watered garden,
>   like a spring whose waters never fail.

4. **LISTEN to a friend.** Brennan Manning says this about addiction:

> For an alcoholic, a "slip" is a terrifying experience. The physical and mental obsession with booze comes like a flash flood in a place everyone thought was high and dry. When the drunk sobers up, he or she is devastated. This is not academic. I'm an alcoholic. My life was ruined by alcohol abuse and restored by the relentless tenderness of Jesus. When I relapsed, I faced two (and only two) options: surrender again to guilt, fear, depression, and maybe death by alcohol, or rush back to the arms of my heavenly Father.[9]

5. **RESPOND to God's nudges.** Try this exercise to break the temptation/attachment cycle:

- *Be self-aware and painfully honest—especially about who we are and what attracts us.* Transparency, transparency, transparency is crucial during this step if we're to change. Our tendency is to save face, justify and excuse our behavior, and reveal only part of the problem. Don't make this mistake. We'd be wise to take off our masks, bare all before

God, and let Him get to the root of the issue. *Begin with some questions:*

> What are my addictions? What are the idols in my life? Do others notice my attachment to these things? Am I willing to accept the truth about them? Do I want to surrender them to Jesus? Do I believe He is able to help me overcome my misplaced desires?

> Are my affections "nailed" to something or someone other than the cross? When things get bad, do I put my trust in Jesus, or retreat to other so-called "safe places"— the arms of some less-than-holy source of power? Does my walk with Christ feel hindered?

- *Remember what God really thinks of us.* As sinners, we are all "children of wrath."[10] Even so, the Lord has forgiven our rebellion against Him. And even while we were still rejecting God, Jesus died for us.[11] He looked down at those who nailed Him to a cross and cried out, "Father, forgive them, for they do not know what they are doing."[12] God wants to forgive our sins so we can spend eternity with Him! (Check out Exodus 34:6–7.)

- *Remember that God is our true father—our heavenly Father.* He loves us, cares for us, equips us, and stands with us in our trials. Understanding who we really are as His children will help give us the courage to be who He created us to be and overcome the Enemy.

- *Find community and transparency with someone we can trust.* We all need someone we can tell our secrets to without feeling judged, someone who genuinely loves and respects us and who will be a consistent presence. This person should be willing to help us walk the path to righteousness. In other words, they should serve as a sponsor or mentor. Start by talking to a pastor or professional therapist. When we do begin meeting with a sponsor, we should be willing to answer these eight transparency questions:

  (1) What known sins have you committed since our last meeting?

  (2) What temptations have you struggled with?

  (3) How were you delivered?

  (4) What have you thought, said, or done that causes your conscience to feel uneasy?

  (5) Is your thought life pure? (Tell what you're doing to protect it or describe how you've blown it.)

  (6) Are you spending time alone with Jesus? (Describe your quiet times or share why you're neglecting them.)

  (7) Are you keeping any secrets?

  (8) Have you lied about any of the previous questions?[13]

- *Feed on the Word of God.* Memorizing and even praying through Scripture is powerful—especially when we're weak and tempted and can't find a way of escape. Speak the name of Jesus when you pray, believing the Word that you're engaging and standing firm on the promises given to you as a daughter or son of God.

- *Clue in to our weaknesses and limits.* This knowledge usually comes to us through experience and failure, and it's important that we learn from our failures and shortcomings. A mentor or an accountability partner can help us look objectively at the relevant areas in our lives. Likewise, God's Spirit will guide us. He will reveal our "hot buttons" as He cleanses us, tearing down our old ways of thinking and renovating our "spiritual house."

6. **PRAY.** Consider expressing this prayer from *The Prisoner's Lantern*:

I do not know how you can deliver me, Lord, but you are the only just and loving God. Give me the Holy Spirit who will free me from bondage—whatever my bondage, whether behind iron bars or not behind bars.[14]

7

Michael's Story: Worried to Death

How Anxiety and Fear Can Be Stumbling Blocks

One minute I (Mike) was laughing and enjoying "Boys' Night" with my son, the next I was pressing a cell phone tightly to my ear, motioning for quiet . . . fighting back tears.

"I don't think I'm going to make it," whispered a raspy voice on the other end. "I've been in and out of the emergency room all week. This time they had to drain fluids out of my chest. I'm back home now, propped up on the couch. Tired. Just sitting here, waiting. . . ."

It was my older brother Jerry. He sounded hoarse; his words were labored. He was medicated again—heavily drugged.

Jerry had cancer.

He'd been battling it for nearly two years—twenty-four hellish months of blood tests, MRIs, CT scans, PET scans, simple X-rays, physical therapies. Poking. Probing. Jabbing. Injecting.

There were constant visits with chemical oncologists, radiologists, pulmonologists; countless surgical procedures and thousands and thousands of dollars spent on drugs—some that appeared to do more harm than good, others that promised to be "the silver bullet" against cancer. Yet despite an all-out medical assault, my once robust brother was steadily withering into listless emaciation, the victim of a terminal illness.

I had to accept what I'd tried hard to deny: Jerry was dying.

"I'm so sorry." I spoke slowly and deliberately. The pizza parlor was loud, and our connection was weak. "I'm so very sorry. I think you can beat this. You've fought so hard."

"I'm tired, Mike . . . very tired." Jerry paused, and then spoke again, seeming a bit more reflective. "I've tried to do some good in this life, to help people, to be there for them—"

"Yes, you have. You've been there for me."

"I don't think I'm going to make it."

"I'll keep praying."

"Pray. Yes—please do. And know that I love you. That's why I called. I just wanted to tell you that."

"I love you too."

"I've got to hang up now . . . got to go."

"Good-bye, Jerry."

"Good-bye."

As my brother's name faded from the screen, I stared at my phone in disbelief. *Is that it? Are those the last words I'll ever say to him?*

I looked up and scanned the restaurant. So many smiling faces— couples and families, first dates and retirees. Just to my right, two middle-aged men in ties were swilling beers and talking business. A grandmother was doting on a toddler to my left. Directly in front of me, a young man and woman were celebrating. *An anniversary? A pregnancy? A first home?*

Everyone all around me was laughing, toasting, talking . . . living.

And then my gaze caught my son's eyes. Ten-year-old Christopher had that deer-in-the-headlights expression. "Daddy, you're sad. Is everything okay?"

I forced a grin. "Yes. Things will be all right. Uncle Jerry is really sick today."

"He's always sick." Christopher picked up a slice of pepperoni pizza and held it awkwardly. "Is he . . . you know—"

"It's hard, but let's talk to Jesus about him. God knows just what to do."

"Okay, Daddy—okay."

Immobilized by Worry and Fear

Suddenly—in the midst of a life fresh and green and full of dreams—death intrudes. Your death. The real thing. *Das ding an sich,* as the Germans say: "The thing itself."[1]

Walter Wangerin Jr. wrote those words in *Letters From the Land of Cancer.* He too was fighting for his life, and he had a lot to say to victims and those who love them. Outwardly, I tried to smile and stay positive, but emotionally I felt as if I were shattering into a million jagged pieces. Wangerin was helping me to understand . . . to prepare.

When we remain unprepared for the Ultimatum certainly to seize us, then the death that interrupts our daily lives is monstrous. Fight against it with all your might. Hate it. Be filled with envy and anger for those who are still healthy. Wail, plead, beg, make deals with friends and with the Infinite. Sink into despair. Lie down in hopelessness. Die, then—even before you die. Or else, prepare. Long before that final confrontation, prepare.[2]

Wangerin was helping me see how anxiety, worry, and fear had become my own cancer—spiritual stumbling blocks stealing from my relationship with Jesus Christ. In a very real sense, I was allowing Jerry to slip away even before he was gone, allowing myself to die even before my life was over.

Anxiety, worry, and fear were robbing me of *life.*

Here's how clinical psychologist Frank Freed defines a love-fear-anger cycle at work in each of our lives:[3]

LOVE: *moves toward a person, place, or thing*

FEAR: *moves away from a person, place, or thing*

ANGER: *moves against a person, place, or thing*

When we keep taking a step forward (love) and then a step backward (fear), we become immobilized and end up going nowhere. This leads to feelings of frustration, which most often are the basis of anger. And anger most often causes us to move against ourselves.

Sometimes I find myself caught up in this cycle. In fact, I've traced it all the way back to my early childhood—right around when my father abandoned my family. (I was just six when it happened.) The cycle grew as I watched my mom worry her way through what must have felt like an impossible job: She had to raise six kids all by herself! I was the youngest and certainly the most high-maintenance of her children.

"Mrs. Ross, that boy of yours is such a worrywart," my first-grade teacher once said during a conference. Then she grabbed my mom's hand. "Is everything okay at home? How are you holding up?"

I held my breath—selfishly worried that Mom would say something that would make us—actually, ME—seem different . . . inferior. *Will my teacher stop liking us? Will the other kids think we're weird?* (As an adult, I've cut myself some slack. After all, first-graders aren't supposed to worry; they're *supposed* to have a childhood.)

Junior high was a nightmare. "Come on, Ross—don't be so scared of the ball," barked Mr. Battle, my PE instructor. (Yep, his name was *Battle*, which ironically described the torment I endured day after day.) "Man up. Put some muscle into it." During those moments, I'd have given anything to melt into the cracks of the gym floor. *Sorry, Mr. Battle, but I don't feel much like a man. Most of the time, I just feel scared.*

College was better. "This boy can write," one professor said—in front of a classroom filled with my peers. And then he proceeded to read something I'd written. It was my first journalism assignment, and my prof was a hard-nosed newsman who seemed otherwise impossible to please. The affirmation built me up . . . until negative self-talk and the love-fear-anger cycle brought me down again. *But what kind of a future will I have? Competition among writers is fierce. And don't most of them starve?*

Marriage brought a phenomenal change for the better. "You know, it's all going to be okay," Tiffany often tells me. "God is in control. Do you actually believe this? All the worry in the world isn't going to change a thing. It won't bring us more money, or make us more acceptable . . . or cure a terminal illness. Can you take a faith step and trust Him with the things that worry you? Can you trust Him enough to release all these fear traps?"

Praise God for godly women! Praise God for life mates we can lean on, for lovers who gently nudge us back to the cross. *She really knows me—the person I am inside . . . worrywart and all—yet she loves me anyway. I don't have to perform or mask my flaws. I'm acceptable just as I am.*

🍎 🍎 🍎

I wish the kind of fear I struggle with was the amusement-park variety.

You know—the type that plays with your adrenaline, tickling your senses shortly after you buckle yourself in on a roller coaster. You're usually pretty confident that nothing worse than losing your lunch will happen. And you're at least somewhat certain that the ride will be over in thirty to sixty seconds, gently delivering you back to that long line where you waited for thirty minutes—just to get scared! Amusement-park fear is a mere imitation of the real thing.

The emotions I've dealt with all these years relate to apprehension, worry, stress, and anxiety. They can range in severity from mere twinges of uneasiness to full-blown panic attacks marked by rapid heartbeat, trembling, sweating, queasiness, and terror. Sometimes these feelings are connected to everyday worries and strike out of the blue (called "free-floating anxiety"). Sometimes they're more out of proportion, even unrealistic, and are triggered by specific struggles (called "situation anxiety").

For example, the abandonment I endured as a child makes me especially sensitive to issues of death and loss. Watching my brother suffer terminally is horribly painful for me. I love him. I don't want him to suffer, and I certainly don't want to lose him. Death and loss are major stress points for everyone, but they're intensified in the lives of those who battle anxiety.

Says Edmund Bourne, who specializes in treatment of anxiety disorders:

> People who suffer from anxiety are especially prone to engage in fearful self-talk. Anxiety can be generated on the spur of the moment by repeatedly making statements to yourself that begin with the two words: *what if.*[4]

Yet God is teaching me to surrender anxiety, worry, and fear—and He's replacing them with faith. A few practical steps are helping me along the way:

Empathy. My wife nudges me closer to God, and He nudges me deeper into His wisdom: "Trust in the LORD with all your heart and lean not on your own understanding."[5] And His wisdom is transformational.

Positive Self-Talk. When I begin to feel immobilized by catastrophic thoughts—"What if nobody likes me?" "What if I fail?" "What if I lose the ones I love?"—I neutralize fear with positive self-talk. For example, I might tell myself something like this:

> **Live; don't live in fear. Relax—and trust**
> **God. Believe in God's truth, not the lies you**
> **are thinking. Know that God is in control.**
> **Be still, and know that HE is God.**[6]

Prayer. I usually have conversations with Jesus throughout the day—as I drive, as I write, before I head into meetings, during prayer and Bible study. I especially pray when anxiety, worry, and fear invade my thoughts. For me, this is the single most effective step. And when anxiety flares, my prayer may go something like this: *Dear Jesus, I need your strength, protection, and truth right now. You know what I'm feeling. Keep Satan away from me. Heal my heart; heal my mind. In your name I pray. Amen.*

God's Word. In chapter 5 Arnie showed how I use spiritual interruptions to combat my struggles. As Scripture is worked into my life, God begins speaking to me intimately—guiding me, changing me. There's a supernatural component to the Bible no one can explain. It has to be experienced.[7]

Empowerment. Through the power of the Holy Spirit I am protected from the Enemy's attacks. I don't have to roll over and play dead. I can overcome anxiety, worry, fear, and any other soul-robbing choice. The truth is we all have a choice. We're responsible for how we feel and behave (barring physiological factors). It's what we say to ourselves in response to any particular situation that mainly determines our mood and emotions.[8]

Control, though, isn't easy to give up—especially in the face of a real (not just imagined) crisis.

A Little Crisis Control, Please!

My wife and I, like most people, can recall exactly where we were when we heard a plane had crashed into one of the World Trade Center towers. And it was when the second plane hit that we were thrown into crisis. What was going on? What were we supposed to do? We looked at each other and felt confused, scared, and angry. Everything seemed to stop as we—and millions of others—watched live coverage of innocent people fighting for their lives. There was mass confusion as panic set in. Thousands faced split-second decisions: *Should I stay where I am or try the fire escape? Should I race for cover here or over there? Should I help someone else—or just run for my life?*

Meanwhile, our leaders were faced with defending our country from any further attacks. *Should we ground all flights? What action should we take if a commercial jet isn't responding properly?*

Before we knew it, cell phones weren't working. The FAA couldn't account for several airplanes. The Pentagon had been hit, the hub of our nation's military and intelligence. A plane was down in Pennsylvania; the stock market ceased; rescue workers found themselves defending their own lives.

Fortunately, several things also went right that day. Our leadership remained safe; our government functioned; the military performed effectively; people throughout the world came to our aid. But the window of horror left me more than shaken. My sense of security had taken a blow. It was hard to catch up with how quickly my world was changing. It was as if, instantly, a mirror had been held up to my life: I was making two of the same mistakes people have made throughout the ages.

Error #1: Believing That Life Is Within My Control

From the beginning of time, humankind has wanted to be the center of the universe. Think back to chapter 1: The root of the love-fear-anger cycle—and the stumbling blocks of anxiety, worry, and fear—started with Adam and Eve in the garden of Eden. God told the world's first couple that He alone was the arbiter of right and wrong. They only had to live as if God's view of good and evil was the right one. And of course it is.

Consider Joseph, for example: He wasn't in control of circumstances, but he *was* in control of his actions.[9] He behaved as if God was in control; therefore, Joseph was able to participate in the amazing work God accomplished and experience the joy that work produced.[10]

Error #2: Fearing That Life Is Spinning Out of Control

In the midst of chaos there's a strong temptation to believe that no one is in control, and this naturally induces fear. After all, just stop and think about all the things that could go wrong today—everything from nuclear accidents to traffic accidents, from scalding coffee to global warming. From too many carbs to killer bees. It's scary out there!

So Who Is Really in Control?

I remember how everyone from news anchors to schoolchildren were offering prayers for the victims and their families on 9/11.

Churches were full, and ministers worked overtime to respond to those in need. When all else failed—people turned to God. Some came in anger and some in confusion, but most of us came with a cry for help.

As my wife reminds me, it all boils down to an issue of trust. *Who, or what, do I run to when the going gets tough?* My trust is misplaced when I depend heavily on human knowledge and ability rather than on my Creator.

Our God is jealous. He has helped us develop the comforts of modern life, but He does not want us to substitute them for our trust in Him. What will it take to get our attention? He longs for us to come to Him constantly.

I don't want to wait until I'm forced out of my comfort zone again to lean on Christ. So I'm striving to let go and trust Him in *every* situation. Believe me, I'm not always successful. Too often pride and fear get in the way. Thankfully our Lord is strong—and very, very patient.

🍎 🍎 🍎

There's so much the Lord is teaching me:

I can TRUST Him in the midst of a crisis. What's more, I'm discovering I can find comfort in the reality that I'm not the one in control. I'm beginning to lean on an old familiar truth:

> "Be still, and know that I am God;
>   I will be exalted among the nations,
>   I will be exalted in the earth."
> The LORD Almighty is with us;
>   the God of Jacob is our fortress.[11]

I can TRUST that He has not abandoned me. In times of distress, I can call out to Him and He will give me the power of His Spirit. He will help me to handle whatever it is that I must face.

I can TRUST His Word when life feels out of control:

> The LORD is good,
> a refuge in times of trouble.
> He cares for those who trust in him.[12]

> Christ also suffered once for sins, the righteous for the unrighteous, to bring you to God.[13]

> God so loved the world that he gave his one and only Son, that whoever believes in him shall not perish but have eternal life.[14]

> Jesus said, "Peace be with you! As the Father has sent me, I am sending you." And with that he breathed on them and said, "Receive the Holy Spirit."[15]

> This is love for God: to keep his commands. And his commands are not burdensome, for everyone born of God overcomes the world.[16]

An Unexpected Phone Call

> Stable. My tumors sleep. The earth turns.
> My Lord is near. I am quiet here—and stable.[17]

It was June 2012—a Tuesday—a few days after Father's Day. My phone rang and *Jerry* flashed on the screen. I paused for a moment, savoring each letter of his name. Then I hit Accept. But before I could say "hello"—

"Michael," a voice interrupted. "It's your brother." Oh, that raspy voice I love so much. It was still labored, but a little less medicated. He continued: "I just wanted to wish you a late Happy Father's Day."

A big smile stretched across my face. Imagine that: My brother, terribly sick, still calls me. He's not giving up; he's *living* . . . celebrating every precious breath he's been given.

"Happy Father's Day to you, my brother," I said. "Has your son been over to see you?"

"Oh—all the time. He's been so good to me!"

"I wish I could be there with you. I wish we didn't have three states between us."

"It's all good, Mike . . . it's all good. Give Tiffany and Christopher a hug. And give yourself one too. I love you, brother."

"I love you too."

"Good-bye for now. . . ."

Then the Angel showed me Water-of-Life River, crystal bright. It flowed from the Throne of God and the Lamb, right down the middle of the street. The Tree of Life was planted on each side of the River, producing twelve kinds of fruit, a ripe fruit each month. The leaves of the Tree are for healing the nations. Never again will anything be cursed. The Throne of God and of the Lamb is at the center. His servants will offer God service—worshiping, they'll look on his face, their foreheads mirroring God. Never again will there be any night. No one will need lamplight or sunlight. The shining of God, the Master, is all the light anyone needs. And they will rule with him age after age after age.[18]

NUDGE SEVEN: Surrender Control

TEMPTED—Identifying Soul-Robbing Traps

The temptation to worry and the stumbling blocks of anxiety and fear have touched my life also. Here's how I've been trapped:

Here's why giving up control is so hard for me:

I'd like Jesus to help me with:

TESTED—Learning How to Break Free

What Research Confirms About Worry and Fear:

A growing number of Americans are battling anxiety, worry, and fear on a daily basis. Most of us engage in fearful self-talk on the spur of the moment, usually beginning with two words: *what if.* Any anxiety we experience in anticipation of confronting a difficult situation is manufactured from our own what-if statements:[19] "What if I fail?" "What if I can't handle the task?" "What if I lose my job, my family . . . my life?" Just *noticing* when we fall into catastrophic thinking is the first step toward surrendering it to God and overcoming this highly detrimental pattern.

A Proven Path:

(1) Give up control.
(2) Engage God-centered self-talk.

The key: Hiding God's Word in our hearts, coupled with prayer. And as Michael demonstrated, we can counter fear and catastrophic thinking by reminding ourselves of the truth.

What Christ-Followers Are Telling Us:

The minute I find myself overcome by worry and fear, and giving in to anxiety and negative self-talk, I stop and pray. And then with God's help, I diffuse the anxiety: "Live in truth. Trust Jesus. He is in control, not me. He will get me through this." I even recite verses like Galatians 2:20.

TRUE—Charting a Path Toward Change

1. *RECEIVE God's Word.* Read or listen to Romans 8:28–39.

2. REFLECT on verses 38–39. Pull them apart sentence by sentence, seeking God's personal message to you. Invite His Spirit to speak.

I am convinced that neither death nor life, neither angels nor demons, neither the present nor the future, nor any powers, neither height nor depth, nor anything else in all creation, will be able to separate us from the love of God that is in Christ Jesus our Lord.

What is God saying to you? After a moment of silence before Him, converse with Him (talk and listen) through prayer.

Begin with general thoughts and impressions . . .

- "Heavenly Father, here's what I feel when I read these verses":

....

....

- "Here's what's hard for me, God—what I don't understand":

....

....

Now relate these verses to your specific struggles:

- "Here's what Romans 8:28–39 is telling me about defeating stumbling blocks like anxiety, worry, and fear":

....

....

....

- "With your help, Lord, here's how I'll endeavor to let go and surrender my life to you":

....

....

....

3. MEMORIZE Romans 8:31–32. Repeat it to yourself as often as needed. Write it out on an index card and post it where you'll see it.

> If God is for us, who can be against us? He who did not spare his own Son, but gave him up for us all—how will he not also, along with him, graciously give us all things?

4. LISTEN to a friend. C. S. Lewis says this about giving up control and surrendering our will to God's will:

> The almost impossible thing is to hand over your whole self—all your wishes and precautions—to Christ. But it is far easier than what you are trying to do instead. For what we are trying to do is remain what we call "ourselves," to keep personal happiness as our great aim in life, and yet at the same time be "good." We are all trying to let our mind and heart go their own way—centered on money or pleasure or ambition—and hoping, in spite of this, to behave honestly and chastely and humbly. And that is exactly what Christ warned us you could not do.[20]

5. RESPOND to God's nudges. Try this courage-building exercise:

- Stand in front of a full-length mirror and evaluate the person you see. As you study that man or woman, ask yourself some questions: *Who am I? Is this the best me? Is there room for improvement? What can I change? What must I accept about myself? What must I let go of? What does God think of me?*

- Consider all the other times you've spent in that very spot, holding in your tummy, rearranging your hair, checking your physique—expending much effort on your appearance so that maybe, just maybe, you'll gain the acceptance of others. Then think about this:

  > *Jesus knows everything about you, yet He's crazy in love with you.* He died so you can spend eternity with Him; He wants you to love (not fear) others the way He loves each of us.[21]

Jesus tells you to stop worrying about life. Let Him take care of all the things that trouble you.[22]

Jesus tells you to let go. He can be trusted; He will catch us and take care of us each time we fall.[23] And yes, we will fall.

- Next, ask yourself this question: What is one step I can take to begin worrying a little less tomorrow? Then tell yourself . . .

  "*I can,* because Jesus set me free to live in wholeness, in fullness—because I've been given fullness in Him."

  "*I can,* because God gives me permission to fail, and He gives me the ability to succeed."

  "*I can,* because God is transforming me from 'spiritual loser' to 'spiritual winner.'"

6. *PRAY.* Tonight, and anytime in the future, consider expressing this prayer by Dietrich Bonhoeffer:

> *O Lord my God, I thank you that you have brought this*
> *day to a close;*
> *I thank you that you have given me peace in body and*
> *soul.*
> *Your hand has been over me and has protected and pre-*
> *served me.*
> *Forgive my puny faith, the ill that I this day have done,*
> *and help me to forgive all who have wronged me.*
> *Grant me a quiet night's sleep beneath your tender care.*
> *And defend me from all the temptations of darkness.*
> *Into your hands I commend my loved ones and all who*
> *dwell in this house;*
> *I commend my body and soul.*
> *O God, your holy name be praised. Amen.*[24]

8

Mark's Story:
Coming Clean With a Secret War

How He's Turning From Sexual Sin

It's late.
Better stop. Well, a few more clicks . . .
Wait—that can't be the time!
I just checked the clock.
Maybe I can't stop.
Or maybe I'm just being uptight.
It's not like I'm hurting anyone.
And my life is stressful. This helps.
But will God forgive me?
What if my wife finds out?
What if she already knows?
Maybe I should stop.
It's so late.
Maybe too late. . . .

By the time Mark graduated from high school, he was living two lives: one secret, one public. *It's like two different people are sharing the same body,* he'd sometimes think. *I'm not sure which one is the real me.*

What captivated his heart was also what he hated most—a monster inside that was causing him to hate himself. Yet he couldn't manage to break free.

At least no one knows.

On the surface, everything looked normal. Better than normal, actually, exceptional. Mark was handsome, and athletic, and likable. He went to college in his hometown, St. Louis. He sang in his church choir and was unofficially nominated as the boy every mom wanted her daughter to marry.

He managed to convince himself that his life was good. Most days were routine, quietly compartmentalized—all within his control, just as he liked it. He learned how to cover his tracks, turn on and off his emotions . . . even somehow dissociate himself from his own secret late-night activities.

Life is *good,* he'd tell himself, *and seems to be getting better and better.*

🍎   🍎   🍎

Mark loved Ashley, his high school sweetheart.[1] And when the two married, he promised to be faithful to her his whole life.

"Nothing will ever come between us," he promised with a kiss. "I love you with all my heart. I *give* you my heart."

Within a few years, Ashley had her hands full with two energetic toddlers. Mark worked long hours to climb the corporate ladder and had big shoes to fill as vice president of international sales. The stress was brutal, but his secret helped him to cope. (That is, that's how he justified his choices and actions.)

Porn had become a soothing after-hours cocktail—one that often turned into a distressing hangover the next morning.

"Why were you up so late—*again?*" Ashley wondered.

"Work, honey. Tons of it. You know the stress I'm under."

"It's always work . . . it's always something. What about me? What about our marriage?"

As much as this family man tried to deny what he was doing, and as much effort as he invested into suppressing what he was hiding, each connection with a voice on his cell phone or a video on his laptop was taking a relational toll. Mark was often too tired for real sex. Like white cotton soaking up black ink, his heart was becoming darker, more distorted. With each hit, the actual man was being replaced by a great pretender, someone who said the right words and smiled at the right times but was merely playing a part.

He was very much addicted, very much trapped, and not just to an image or to a fantasy. He had a full-blown addiction to adrenaline—to taking a porn hit that delivered a feel-good signal whenever he decided he needed one.

🍎 🍎 🍎

One day, Mark hastened the collapse of his increasingly tenuous situation with another kind of misstep.

"I'm sorry, Ashley, but I can't work for you anymore," blurted the housekeeper through her barely opened minivan window. Her hands were trembling; she'd been crying. "Call the agency—they'll send a replacement."

Ashley's face creased. Then she frowned. "But I don't understand. You're like family to us." She was very young, and a single mom, and needed the work. Ashley had hoped she could keep taking her under her wing.

"Can we talk about this?" she continued, pleading. "Could you tell me what's wrong? I care about you, and I really don't want to lose you."

But suddenly the front door opened, and Mark stuck his head out. "Honey, is everything okay?"

The housekeeper hit the gas and sped away from the curb. Ashley practically had to leap aside.

She turned and locked eyes with Mark. *Late nights in the home office. No interest in romance. Now Candice is terrified? It's all beginning to add up.*

Her mind began to run wild. Then she shuddered at the thought of what might have happened. Trust was on the line, and so was their marriage.

Ashley knew the painful steps she had to take, but she couldn't imagine taking them alone. She needed help.

Mountain-Sized Confrontation

At any other time a ski trip with Jake would've been a welcome getaway. His minister was like a second dad to him. But Mark was suspicious. The way Ashley had orchestrated the whole thing and then insisted that he go—

They obviously know something, Mark thought. *The house-keeper talked.*

Then he began to build his case. *I'm innocent. I didn't lay a finger on her. SHE actually walked in on ME—invading MY privacy. Nothing happened. Okay, maybe what I said was a little off-color . . . but it was a joke; who wouldn't want to diffuse an embarrassing situation? If anyone should be apologizing, it's her. This whole thing is getting way out of proportion.*

After a day of carving up Vail Mountain, the subject hadn't come up. Jake and Mark had talked about practically everything else—work, stress, raising kids, childhood memories. Over dinner the previous night, Mark had found himself opening up about his dad and their strained relationship. "I've always been a disappointment to him," he'd admitted. "I can't seem to please him. 'You're a screw-up,' he said when I was twelve. I could never live up to his standards."

Around lunchtime the following day, the pair coasted into Two Elk Chili, high atop the mountain. Hearty buffalo burgers and a spectacular view seemed a perfect combo, and the restaurant was nearly empty. But just as Mark took a bite, Jake dropped a bomb. "You sure were up late again. That happen often?"

Mark looked up and swallowed. "Yeah. Catching up on some emails and work issues. You know—the life of corporate sales. And then I was playing a few computer games, they usually help me unwind."

"Or maybe you were playing with fire?"

"Fire?"

"Porn, Mark. It can destroy everything, and everyone, in its path."

Ashley knows. So does he. But it wasn't the thought of fire that shot heat through every cell of his being. *How could they dupe and trap me like this?*

He remained silent.

Jake sipped hot tea and leaned forward. "You ever see your wife as God's gift to you?"

Mark nodded, tentatively.

"Me too. That's how I see Lauren. I wanted someone sweet and loving right beside me—a friend and lover who'd believe in me no matter what, who'd be with me always. Most of us guys want a faithful woman to respect us and trust us. And we sure don't complain if she's beautiful."

Here comes the sermon. Yeah, I get it, I get it . . . I'm a screw-up.

"I knew she was the one as soon as I met her. I wanted to protect her and take care of her—I actually thought of myself as her knight in shining armor."

Mark couldn't help rolling his eyes. *Is he rubbing my nose in his SHINY morals?* "Congrats on finding perfection." He heard the venom in his voice.

"It's been far from perfect, Mark. I nearly lost her. I nearly lost everything. Mark, listen to me: For years, I kept a mistress."

Mark's head snapped back. His eyes flamed; his nostrils flared. Quickly he stood to his full height. "No, you listen to me, Jake. Okay? I did something stupid, in my office. Our housekeeper opened the door . . . but I didn't do anything—I didn't so much as touch her. And *I* have *not* cheated on my wife."

Jake tried to reach across. "Mark, let me finish. Can you hear me out?"

Mark's whole body was shaking. Breathing rapidly, he turned away and tasted the salt from his tears. When he felt his pastor's hand on his shoulder he didn't shrug it off, but his posture stayed rigid. "How could *you* be unfaithful? . . . And you're trying to say I'm the same way?" His voice began rising again. "Who's the real hypocrite here, Jake?"

Rage rose in him, and he turned back around. "You're our pastor—our spiritual leader—and yet you've acted like a fraud?"

Jake nodded. "What you're saying is true. All of it. And I'm so sorry."

Mark blinked. "You're *sorry?* But *why?* How could you do this to her? Lauren trusted you. She LOVES you."

Jake leaned back. "I love her too, Mark. But I thought I could have it both ways. I wouldn't listen; I ignored the warnings. I didn't want to believe having a mistress would create problems, much less wreak havoc."

Mark looked incredulous. "*How* could you think *that?*"

"My mistress was pornography."

As his pastor looked deeply into his eyes, and as his words sunk into his heart, Mark felt defensive. He sat down. "What I do online isn't real."

Jake took his chair also. "There's a sense in which you've got that right. Porn is a counterfeit that can ruin our ability to experience the real thing."

"Well, it's not like having a real mistress or anything. It's not like I'm going to prostitutes or trying to meet up with actual women."

"It isn't? You mean, it's not like 'having sex'? Think about what you're saying, Mark—you're trying to carve out disconnected realms for the physical and spiritual and emotional, as if each of us is really several different people. Living that way tears us apart inside; that's what I mean about damaging ourselves, wrecking our ability to have the real thing by cutting off our own selves from what we experience. Jesus said that if I look at a woman with lust, I'm committing adultery. It's not just a 'rule'—that's the fact of what I'm doing to myself and how I'm treating others.

"I was foolish in so many ways, Mark. I closed my eyes and ears, my heart and mind, to the truth—that's why I wasn't realizing that gradually I was destroying myself and hurting everyone around me, my wife most of all. When I married Lauren, I actually didn't see that my habit would affect our marriage—that it would numb my feelings, deaden my heart, darken my mind, and poison my love for her." He cleared his throat, then continued. "I thought I could have her, have a normal life, *and* my porn. I was so wrong."

"Meaning?"

"It got to where my addiction so invaded our relationship—I became so twisted . . ." Jake stopped. His shoulders begin to shake.

"Pastor?"

Jake looked out the window. Seconds passed as he fought for control. "Finally, she had had enough. I had to choose. I was at the brink of losing her."

*   *   *

As both men retreated into their thoughts and they settled their tab, an argument began forming in Mark's mind. *Porn itself doesn't hurt anyone. Every guy looks at this stuff. I can control it. Maybe he couldn't, but I can.*

He headed outside for his skis and followed the ridge to a slow green run, relieved that Jake didn't come after him. He needed time to think.

Porn had become his friend, his comfort, his escape. He'd never considered it "bad." As long as you didn't start having sex with other people, it was harmless, a normal, everyday male activity, the next best thing when Ashley wasn't in the mood—which, lately, seemed to be the norm.

But now that I think about it, I'm the one who's not in the mood—too tired, too stressed . . . too enamored with my "friend"?

Porn's always "in the mood"—if it came down to an invite from both, would I choose Ashley? How can porn not be affecting my marriage if I'm asking myself this? . . .

Mountain Wisdom

Later on, they stood side by side, looking down on Vail Village. It felt good to talk openly with a guy who really understood. "Sometimes I feel pulled."

"I know," Jake said. "And the pull keeps getting stronger, doesn't it. At the start I felt I could walk away when I chose. But as time went on, I felt more and more like I was up to my neck in quicksand."

Mark nodded. "Yeah—and I want more all the time. Harder stuff too."

Jake slipped off his shades and squinted at the snow-covered valley. "That's because porn is a true addiction. You need more and more to get a high. You feel you can't live without the buzz.

Before you realize what's happened, it consumes everything—you begin to live for the next encounter."

"But Pastor, I know I'm a Christian."

Jake looked into his eyes. "Yes. But when you find yourself going to porn to meet your needs, then it's become an idol. The Lord won't accept any other gods before Him. You can't have it both ways. You have to make a choice."

"Sometimes I feel I don't have one."

"But you do. God gave you the freedom to choose."

"Then how do I stop?"

"God has given us the power to decide, but only He is strong enough to make the rescue—we can't deliver ourselves." Jake slipped his glasses back on. "Watching some of these new skiers tumble out of control makes me think of how I was once caught in an avalanche. After the elements took over, I was being pulled along against my will. I was being buried alive."

Mark grimaced. "Not now, though, right?"

Jake smiled. "Not for four years. I cried out to Him, and He rescued me."

I need to be rescued too. "So, that's it? I have to pray?"

"It's the place to start. There are two other needs. You have to want to be free—be willing to turn away and give up the habit. You ready to do that?"

"Yes."

"Say it."

Mark swallowed. "I want to give up my porn habit."

"Good."

"What else?"

"Admit you can't do it alone. There's no way I'd have kicked the habit by myself—I needed others to pull me out of the onslaught, help me, walk with me, and hold me accountable. Now I'm free, and I'm making sure our church helps others who are caught in the avalanche."

Mark began to tremble. "Will you help me, Pastor?"

Jake reached over and pulled him close. "Yes, I will—*and Jesus will.*"

Relief flooded Mark. Suddenly he felt like that twelve-year-old boy being held safely in the welcoming arms of his dad.

The path ahead wouldn't be easy. But he knew it, and he chose it.

🍎 🍎 🍎

Are otherwise emotionally healthy men with a strong sex drive abnormal? Absolutely, positively *NO*. Some may produce a little more testosterone than others, but the bottom line is, an average male has a powerful desire for sex.

Are men with an addiction to pornography in trouble? Absolutely, positively *YES*. A man's desire for sex is not the problem—the problem is the desire's contamination or distortion. "Abnormality" has to do with how men seek to express this drive—what satisfies it and what doesn't. It's here that something terrible happens to our sexuality. Pornography distorts sex. It's addictive, it's sinful, and it's deadly.

Know this also: Most Christian men face a lifelong struggle with their sexuality. Basically, this war is between their hormones and their calling—between still experiencing the fallenness of the human condition and their ongoing need to submit themselves to the purifying power of God's Spirit.

"God-fearing men have a greater struggle than other men, for obvious reasons," explains noted psychologist Dr. Archibald D. Hart. "In fact, godless men don't see the problem. 'Sex is all good,' many say. 'We've just messed it up by infecting it with too many "standards."' If the devil had his way, the whole world would believe sex to be a free-for-all playground without any consequences or repercussions."*

---

* Dr. Archibald D. Hart, quote acquired by Michael Ross during a phone conversation (June 1995). We highly recommend Dr. Hart's book *The Sexual Man* (Nashville: Thomas Nelson, 1995).

A Path to Healthy Sexuality

We need to seriously consider the present state of male sexuality and design better ways to love our wives and raise our children. We need to embrace healthier attitudes, emotions, and actions. We'll never achieve a healthier society while male sexuality is out of control even among believers.

The apostle Paul gave us this timeless prescription:

> It is God's will that you should be sanctified: that you should avoid sexual immorality; that each of you should learn to control your own body in a way that is holy and honorable, not in passionate lust like the pagans, who do not know God.[2]

Like a high-spirited stallion, the sex drive's powerful force must be brought under the Lord's control to become the beautiful thing He intended.

Take a long and honest look at your sexuality. Then accept God's forgiveness and stop flogging yourself for your sexual failures. Persistent guilt and shame make it difficult to shed struggles of any nature, and nowhere more so than in this area, which is so intrinsic to the essence of how God created us.

🍎 🍎 🍎

Here's a way forward that I (Arnie) recommend.

Take the First Step: Admit Your Problem

Issues with lust and porn are nearly always accompanied by deceit. In other words, we make wrong choices to take wrong actions yet convince ourselves we're by no means in the wrong. Remember these words from Patrick Means?[3] "When we want something bad enough, we'll deceive whoever we have to in order to get it. And the first person we have to deceive is ourselves" (by believing the twin lies: "I don't really have a problem" and "I can handle this alone").[4]

Take the Second Step: Give God a Chance

As you go to Jesus Christ in prayer, unload your secrets, your sins, and your shame. Tell Him every detail—just as if He didn't know a thing. Spend some time today reflecting on your struggle—whatever it is that has trapped you. Consider following this timeless advice from Peter Marshall:

> In [your conversation with Christ], be absolutely honest and sincere. Hold nothing back. Our minds are sometimes shocked when we permit our hearts to spill over, but it is good for our souls when we do. If we would only have the courage to take a good look at our motives for doing certain things, we might discover something about ourselves that would melt away our pride and soften our hearts so that God could do something with and for us.[5]

Take the Third Step: Choose to Live Without Secrets

Everyone has problems. However, some know it and don't try to conceal it. Some try to convince themselves *and* others they have no issues. And many know they have problems just like everybody else but try to keep secret anything they believe would tarnish the image they seek to project.

To break it down further, there really are two types of people in this regard: those whose problems aren't hidden and those who attempt to haul around secrets. Sadly, way too many Christian guys try to live in the second category, which in the end only serves to land them in the first, and usually at an awful cost: broken trust, shipwrecked relationships, ruined credibility. Don't let a secret come back to bite you. Make the change now.

Take the Fourth Step: Repent

Once you've confessed the sin and asked Jesus to help you change (this is called repentance), you are to stop flogging yourself. You're completely forgiven. Now—your relationship with God fully restored—you can walk toward growth and change. His Spirit wants to help you. *Invite* the Holy Spirit to help you, and continue inviting Him to help you; submitting your will to God's and inviting His will to be done in you progressively breaks down your resistance and leaves you more and more open to His leading and direction. He *will* help you.

Take the Fifth Step: Get Help

So many of us guys have shed tears of sorrow, promised God we'll never again commit a certain sin . . . and then, a few weeks, days, or even hours later—when temptation builds to a fever pitch—have found ourselves falling right back into the same sin. "When it comes to giving up a secret life," Means says, "I believe there is a simple test to help us know whether we're experiencing true or false repentance. If I'm willing to tell someone else what I'm struggling with and ask for help, then it's true repentance. If I'm not willing to tell anyone else, I'm only fooling myself."[6]

NUDGE EIGHT: Shake the Shame

TEMPTED—Identifying Soul-Robbing Traps

My struggles push me into a toxic shame cycle. Here's how I've been trapped:

_____

_____

Here's why breaking free has been so hard for me:

_____

_____

I'd like Jesus to help me with:

_____

_____

_____

_____

TESTED—Learning How to Break Free

What Research Confirms About Toxic Shame's Effects:

I'm hopeless—too far gone—and simply cannot change. I am what I am and will always be this way. Ever catch yourself thinking these thoughts? If so, you could be trapped in a *toxic shame cycle.* This is quite different from guilt. *Guilt* has to do with our behavior, what we do; *shame* has to do with our identity, who we are. Patrick Means explains:

> When we do something wrong, our God-given conscience rings an alarm. That pang we feel is guilt. Guilt is not destructive to our person because we can do something about it. We can acknowledge our wrongdoing, change our behavior, experience forgiveness, and we no longer have to feel guilty. . . . [Shame] pools and swirls outside the fringes of our lives like a poisonous nerve gas, waiting for us to open the door a crack and let it seep in to paralyze and destroy. Shame, in this sense, is a demotivator for ongoing growth. It usually results in self-condemnation, discouragement, and the urge to give up.[7]

A Proven Path:

(1) Reveal your secrets.
(2) Shake the shame.

Even when we desperately want to change, toxic shame eats away at our core. We end up feeling so flawed, we conclude we're hopeless and worthless and worthy only of rejection—"There isn't an ounce of good left in me," we tell ourselves. And we remain trapped in the cycle. According to Robert S. McGee, toxic shame causes us to expect the worst from ourselves because we believe that's who we are inside: "We're not surprised when we disappoint people because deep down inside we know we're no good."[8]

The answer: Let go of it. We must expose the battle that's being waged inside us—first to God, and then to a trusted friend. We surrender it to Jesus and allow Him to destroy it.

What Christ-Followers Are Telling Us:

Self-hate plunges us deeper into our struggles. And, for me, it always begins with shame. I start feeling alone, isolated—perverted. Way beyond God's love. *I'm depraved, a mess, a loser . . . simply no good and of no use to God.* That's what I'd tell myself. And when you start thinking that way, it's easier to justify "deviant" behavior. *I AM a deviant, so why not give in? What should hold me back? At least this gives me pleasure.* These are all lies. This whole line of reasoning—the toxic shame cycle itself—will lead us to only one place: death.

TRUE—Charting a Path Toward Change

1. RECEIVE God's Word. Read or listen to Titus 3:1–11.

2. REFLECT on verses 3–7. Pull them apart sentence by sentence, seeking God's personal message to you. Invite His Spirit to speak.

We lived in malice and envy, being hated and hating one another. But when the kindness and love of God our Savior appeared, he saved us, not because of righteous things we had done, but because of his mercy. He saved us through the washing of rebirth and renewal by the Holy Spirit, whom he poured out on us generously through Jesus Christ our Savior, so that, having been justified by his grace, we might become heirs having the hope of eternal life.

What is God saying to you? After a moment of silence before Him, converse with Him (talk and listen) through prayer.

Begin with general thoughts and impressions . . .

- "Heavenly Father, here's what I feel when I read these verses":

_____

_____

- "Here's what's hard for me, God—what I don't understand":

_____

_____

Now relate these verses to your specific struggles:

- "Here's what Titus 3:1–11 is telling me about shaking the shame in my life, giving up secrets, and finally living—cleansed and free in Jesus":

_____

_____

- "With your help, Lord, here's what I'm thinking about how I can overcome my soul-robbing choices":

_____

_____

_____

3. **MEMORIZE Titus 3:5–6.** Repeat it to yourself as often as needed. Write it out on an index card and post it where you'll see it.

He saved us through the washing of rebirth and renewal by the Holy Spirit, whom he poured out on us generously through Jesus Christ our Savior, so that, having been justified by his grace, we might become heirs having the hope of eternal life.

4. LISTEN to a friend. John Wesley tells of how we are saved from lugging around a guilty conscience:

All who are partakers of the salvation which is by faith are saved from the guilt of all past sin. All the world is guilty before God . . . there is none who could stand before Him. . . . Yet now the righteousness of God—which is by faith of Jesus Christ—is revealed unto all who believe. Now they are justified freely by His grace, through the redemption that is in Jesus Christ. This Jesus has God set forth to be a propitiation, a complete satisfaction for our sins, through faith in His blood, to demonstrate His righteousness by the forgiveness of sins previously committed. . . . He wiped out the handwriting that was against us, taking it out of the way, nailing it to His cross. And so, there is therefore now no condemnation to those who believe in Christ Jesus.[9]

5. RESPOND to God's nudges. Try this exercise to nurture a shame-free heart:

- *First, identify your main "shame traits."* Chances are one or more accurately describes you—how you think, the way you're wired. If you dig in to the reasons why you think and behave in these ways, you'll likely discover that their roots go all the way back to your childhood. Perhaps as a kid you were constantly told you were worthless, which caused you to feel inferior. Or, conversely, maybe you were labeled *gifted* and were pressured into becoming an overachiever. Maybe you began thinking you had to perform to be "acceptable" to others. Or, the adults in your life could have consistently disregarded your feelings and personal boundaries. Each such scenario can (1) affect your self-image and (2) feed into the toxic shame cycle. Review the Shame Characteristics list and mark the statements that apply to you. In the lines provided, list some specific examples of behaviors and emotions you believe are associated with them.[10]

Shame Characteristics	Specific Examples and Emotions
Low self-confidence, persistent negative feelings about self	
Performance-driven, preoccupied with what others think; people-pleaser	
Unawareness of personal boundaries	
"Martyr syndrome": Sacrificing personal needs, then making others feel guilty about it	
Often numb/out of touch with feelings	
Perfectionism, constantly striving at unrealistic standards	
Frequent or persistent fatigue	
Addictive behavior: impulsive, values nonconformity, have sense of social alienation and heightened stress[11]	
Distrust of people	
Possessiveness in relationships	
Manipulative, with strong need to be in control of self and of others	

God can heal our damaged self-confidence, and His Word shows us the traits that will replace shame. "Only His view of us fills the need we have for a parent to affirm and accept us unconditionally," explains Means. "We need to stop looking to others—our wives, friends, children, bosses—to give us a sense of personal worth."[12] Instead, he says, it's time to believe what God thinks of us: "Greater love has no one than this: to lay down one's life for one's friends."[13] He did this, for us.

- *Next, evaluate where you are at this point in your spiritual life and where you'd like to be in the near future.* Take a look at our Spiritual Life Rating Scale.[14] Reflect on the five lists and answer the questions below. Be honest as you evaluate. Most of us are experts at masking, denying, and suppressing how we really feel. And many men describe themselves as "out of touch" with their feelings. In public, we often try to show our best face, projecting someone very different from the person on the inside.

SPIRITUAL LIFE RATING SCALE

1 Skeptic	2 Seeker	3 Believer	4 Grace-Filled	5 Servant- Minded
Skeptical about Christianity; rejects God's teachings (Matt. 7:26)	Seeking faith; pre-salvation; acting on innate thirst for spirituality (Psalm. 42:1)	Committed to Christ, yet lacks maturity (1 Cor. 3:1–2)	Rooted, built up and growing in God (Col. 2:7)	A sanctified servant; spiritually mature and "others-centered" (Titus 1:1)
Fears death and is unsure about the afterlife	Believes in the afterlife; may believe that eternity is based on how well they behave or that there are multiple paths to heaven / eternity	Believes in eternal life through Christ, yet sometimes doubts personal salvation	Focused on eternity; trusts personal salvation through Christ despite fleeting emotions	Has confident assurance of eternal life through Christ
Feels immobilized and neutralized by struggles	Struggles daily with temptation	Struggles frequently with temptation	Strives to overcome soul-robbing choices through Christ's power; stumbles occasionally, but quickly confesses and repents	Usually victorious over soul-robbing choices through Christ's power; committed to confession and repentance
Rejects God's laws and follows worldly standards	Embraces a variety of religious worldviews	Sometimes lives by worldly standards despite knowing right from wrong	Seeks to live the "fruit of the Spirit" (Gal. 5:22-23); growing in obedience to Christ	Rejects worldly standards, pursues relationship with Christ and obeys His teachings
Rejects Scripture; biblically illiterate	Has encountered God's Word, but is skeptical about the authority of the Bible; biblically illiterate	Trusts God's Word, but rarely reads it; possesses very little Bible knowledge	Engages God's Word four or more times a week; trusts the authority of Scripture; knowledgeable of Bible truths	Engages God's Word daily; trusts the authority of Scripture and applies it to life; knowledgeable of Bible truths
Rarely prays, but quick to blame God	Occasionally prays, but is often hesitant about committing life to Christ	Inconsistent prayer times	Prays daily for others and for self	Prays daily for others; embraces the Body of Christ with agape (sacrificial, servant-type) love

1 Skeptic	2 Seeker	3 Believer	4 Grace-Filled	5 Servant-Minded
Dissatisfied with life	Restless; yearns for "something more"	Overall average life; sometimes happy, sometimes sad	Mostly satisfied with life; striving to make a difference	Generally satisfied with life; fulfilled
Often filled with regrets	Often wrestles with past wounds; struggling; needs reassurance	Striving to overcome regrets; desires transformation	Letting go of past mistakes and healing through Christ; desires to model His grace	Embraces Christ's forgiveness; experiencing genuine transformation
Lacks direction; confused	Turns to various spiritual practices for enlightenment (often false religions and cults); does not yet trust the gospel of Jesus Christ	Still trying to make life work without God in the center; often looks to others for direction	Turns to God's Word for guidance	Growing in wisdom and guided by the Holy Spirit
Often feels anxious; rarely at peace	Often feels uneasy and anxious despite spiritual quests	Doesn't fully rely on God's power; attempts to solve problems through human effort	Mostly relaxed and free of tension	Joyous; at peace with God

Column #___ most accurately describes my faith today.

Key negative feelings I'm dealing with include:

_____

_____

_____

Key positive feelings I'm enjoying include:

_____

_____

_____

Here's what I'd like God to change in me:

Column #___ describes how I'd like my faith to be.
Here are some positive feelings I'd like God to nurture in me:

- *Now let's put it all together.* Plot a course to move you toward emotional and spiritual health, a path marked by transparency, a clear sense of who you are, a realistic sense of your soul-robbing hot buttons, and an idea of how you want to grow in Jesus.

Begin with these three steps:

    (1) Discern how God sees you from how you see yourself.

    (2) De-shame your inner self-talk.

    (3) Replace old core beliefs with new ones.

Reflect on this chart, then fill out responses below:

Old Core Beliefs	New Core Beliefs
At my core I'm bad—unworthy, irredeemable, beyond God's grace.	I am valued—worthwhile and loved by God.
No one will accept or love me as I am.	I am accepted and loved just as I am.
My need for _____ (sex, affirmation, acceptance, wealth, etc.) controls me; I cannot break free from its power.	Jesus Christ, not _____, controls my life; through Him I am set free from sin, addiction, and shame.

Here's what God thinks about me—what's TRUE:
Romans 5:8:

Hosea 2:20:

John 15:12–13:

Psalm 139:13–16:

Based upon what I've explored in this chapter and the questions I've answered above, here are the healing steps I'll take in the days ahead (including the negative emotions and soul-robbing choices I'll hand over to God):

6. **PRAY.** Consider expressing this prayer for healing from *Common Prayer: A Liturgy for Ordinary Radicals*:

In the name of the Father, and of the Son, and of the Holy Spirit, we enjoin your divine mercies. Lord, why do we suffer? Why do we hurt? Shall our only answer be the whirlwind of unknowing that engulfed Job? Why do the wicked flourish, while the righteous waste away? I am left speechless, left with the words "I will trust in you, my God."

God, we ask for the sending of your healing Spirit, who came to us through Jesus, as he breathed upon his disciples. This Spirit gathered your people, to be warmed by the fire of divine presence. By this warmth, may (name of person here) be healed and taken into your care.

Like the blind man whom Jesus healed, may (name of person here) become a sign of your glory, calling you the Anointed One, the one who also anoints us and points us to the love of God. Grant us your healing peace. Amen.[15]

9

Danielle's Story:
Am I *Struggling*, or Am I
Just Plain *Defeated*?

Releasing the Past and Embracing the Future

I (Danielle) showed up at the dorm on the west side of campus.
The room was dark and though it wasn't an official party—not one
that had been announced or generated formal invitations—it was
like most every party in every college in every part of the world.
People flirted and drank and smoked and "hooked up" in various
corners of the small room. Music played low, and the percussive
sound of the bass was like a heartbeat in that space.

I didn't smoke or drink. That wasn't my thing. I remember I
ate pizza that night, topped with pineapple and ham. The cheese
had stuck to the inside of the lid as the delivery guy made his way
across town to our impromptu gathering. I sat on the floor, cross-
legged, and chewed the doughy crust.

There must have been a conversation about playing Truth or
Dare. I don't remember anyone mentioning it, or planning it, or

checking to see if everyone wanted to play. But the rest of the group joined me and we became a circle of boys and girls, trying to be adults, sitting on the floor in the dark.

That game wasn't my thing either—too risky. Someone could look my way and say, "Truth or dare?" and I'd have to pick one. If I chose "truth," the questioner could ask me anything at all, and I'd have to tell the absolute truth. If I chose "dare," I'd have to do whatever he or she challenged. Sometimes you could play an entire game without anything going wrong. But usually it turned sour. Entire reputations could be ruined in one go of Truth or Dare.

If someone had asked, I'd have said "not interested." In my experience, nothing good had ever come from that party game. But it was too late to back out now, not without looking as if I had something to hide. So I sat there and willed things never to come my way. I hoped my only role that night would be to fill a spot in that little circle of people.

I decided the best way to get through would be to play it safe. I'd try to be invisible. If I absolutely had to ask someone which *they* would choose, I'd be nice. If they opted for "truth," I'd ask the name of their favorite movie. If they dared to "dare," I'd make them stand on their head or eat a raw egg—something that wouldn't make me a target in return.

It was a reasonable strategy. But of course it didn't work that night.

There was a boy sitting across from me. He was handsome and talented and popular, the kind of guy anyone would have felt fortunate to be seen with. When the game turned his way and it was time for him to pick someone from the circle, I fixed my eyes on the empty pizza box in the middle of the floor. It leered back at me with a grease-stained grin, and I knew this wouldn't end well. The guy said my name, and I tightened my gaze on that box.

"Truth or dare?" he asked.

I wished I could just say "Pass." But that wasn't an option. I decided I didn't want to have to get up from my spot. Somehow it seemed things would be safer if I could stay put. And besides, he was nice. What would it hurt to just answer him?

"Truth," I said.

There was a split second when I thought he might go easy on me, and then he spoke his question. In front of that group, he didn't ask me about smoking or drinking or movies or raw eggs. He asked me about the thing in my life I knew was wrong but kept doing anyway.

The Excruciating Truth

I'd grown up in church. When I was nine, I'd waded into the baptismal pool in front of our entire congregation. The pastor had put a wooden chair from one of the Sunday school classes into the water. When I got to the middle of that pool, he'd reached out and lifted me up so I could stand on that chair. Without it, the people in the pews wouldn't have been able to see me.

We'd practiced this, the pastor and I. I knew when to say "I do" and then cross my arms over my chest and squeeze my nostrils closed between my thumb and index finger. The water had closed over my face as he lowered me under its surface, and afterward I'd gotten to eat the little cube of bread and drink the tiny glass of grape juice from the silver tray passed down the aisle.

When I was nine, I'd said yes to Jesus. And I'd meant it.

I still meant it, sitting there in that room, in that circle of people, staring at that empty pizza box, with that question hanging above me in the air. The boy wanted to know what I did with guys when we were alone in the dark. How I wished I'd chosen "Dare."

Sex was my thing. How many times had I promised—again—
that the last time was truly *the* last time? That I would wait until I
was married, that never again would I give my body over to a man
who was not my husband. But then I'd find myself making excuses
and rationalizing why this time didn't count, or was different, or
that maybe this guy really would be my husband one day . . . and
didn't that make it all right?

Sex was my thing, and sitting there on that dorm room floor, I told
the ugly truth and let the game move on to the next person. I don't
remember whether he or she picked truth or dare, because I felt as
if I'd just taken off my clothes in front of everyone *and* shown them
the grime that clung to my pores and had embedded itself under
my toenails and filled up my nostrils and caked itself to the roots
of the hair on my scalp. I may have said yes to Jesus all those years
before, but somehow I'd been defeated by sin. It had stuck itself to
me in the same way that cheese stuck to the inside of the pizza box.

The Truth About Us All

There's a funny little prayer that's made its way around online:

> *Dear Lord,*
> *So far today I've done all right. I haven't gossiped, haven't*
> *lost my temper, haven't been greedy, grumpy, nasty, selfish,*
> *or over-indulgent. I'm very thankful for that. But in a few*
> *minutes, God, I'm going to get out of bed. And from then*
> *on, I'm probably going to need a lot more help.*
> *Amen.*

This could be my prayer every day, and it would never get old.
The truth is that my natural inclination is to do the wrong thing.
Left to my own devices, the wrong thing is what comes easy to me.

🍎   🍎   🍎

Unfortunately, I don't get a day off from sin. Sin is one of those things I confront all the time. It trips me up when I'm not looking, and—if I'm not careful—I can let it get the best of me. Sometimes, however, I don't even realize I've been derailed until I begin to notice a subtle nagging in the back of my mind. It makes me feel as if something is just a little bit *off*. I try to press on through my day, but that nagging keeps working its way to the top of my agenda until I just have to stop and deal with it.

This is what I was thinking about the other day as Stacey drove down the highway with me in the passenger seat. We get together twice a month for lunch. When she added the meeting notice to my calendar at work, she named it "Accountability Lunch." We'd talked about it and agreed we needed someone who could keep us in check as we tried to navigate the day-to-day of corporate life while keeping our faith and our integrity intact.

For me, it's easy to slip into those places where popular opinion lies. To make myself look good, it's not so difficult to shift blame or to make someone else look bad. It's a constant struggle. And if I'm not careful, I'll slip.

So Stacey and I get together to share and pray and keep things honest.

That day, we drove into our downtown area and Stacey slowed with the rest of the traffic. We turned left at the corner and started looking for parking spots—no easy task on a weekday at lunchtime. With our city in the throes of a few major construction projects, many of the spots were blocked with orange cones and construction vehicles taking up multiple spaces. We turned one more corner and found a spot. I dropped quarters into the meter.

The wind was strong as we made our way to the restaurant. We walked quickly, and I held my coat closed at my neck, where the wind had found a way around the knot I'd tied in my scarf.

Inside, the sign told us to seat ourselves, and we found a booth in the back. The waitress was friendly and efficient; I ordered a cup of soup with half a sandwich. Then we leaned in over the table.

We talked about Stacey's new baby and plans I have for an upcoming retreat. When our food came, we prayed together and then dug in. My soup was amazing, and the sandwich hit the spot. I wiped the corners of my mouth with my napkin, and then we talked about the places where we struggle.

I confessed the root of the feeling that had been nagging me for the past few hours. I realized it stemmed from my working relationship with Mitch, a colleague. He and I had been working together on a project, and I found it difficult not to belittle him or to roll my eyes when others talked about him.

I'm not the only one. And maybe that's part of the problem. Maybe, because others see him as difficult to work with, I feel justified in joining the bandwagon and adding my testimony to the campaign against him. Honestly, it doesn't take much for me to slip over the edge of that slippery cliff.

Knowing that someone else knows where I struggle is like holding up a mirror and seeing my sin for what it really is. It was no longer just words, or a nagging feeling that I should be doing something different. Now it was a commitment and a desire to actually follow through.

🍎　🍎　🍎

Naturally, my new resolve was tested just a few days later, when I sat in a meeting with Mitch. We walked our way through the tasks on our list, and then I closed my folder and got ready to leave.

"Doing anything fun this weekend?" I heard myself say. It was just one of those questions you ask to be nice and to make the end of the meeting tidy.

"No. Not really," Mitch said. "I'll probably just come in here and get some work done."

I remembered it was a football weekend, so I asked, "No football?"

"I don't have cable. In fact, one weekend I came in here to see if I could watch a game on the TV in the conference room. But that didn't work."

It dawned on me right then that Mitch is just an ordinary guy. Like me, Mitch is just trying to make his way through life without getting stepped on.

"You know," I heard again, and I could barely believe the words myself, "one weekend you should come over and watch the game with my husband and me at our house."

Right Here, Right Now

It's up close and personal, this struggle. I think that's what always surprises me most—that I find myself toe to toe with the temptations that want to get the best of me. Don't get me wrong. I'm not afraid of confrontation. I know how to fight fair. I know how to claim my feelings and own my part in a disagreement. But this opponent doesn't fight fair. Temptation is big, and it's sneaky, and it knows my weak spots. It can tell when I'm wavering and slip in a zinger at just the perfect moment—sending me right back to square one.

It doesn't have to be that way. More and more, I realize there *is* a way out.

Tuning In

A few weeks ago, I sat next to my husband at the back of a plane and buckled myself in. We were on the last leg of a journey, and I was looking forward to being home. I leaned my head back against the seat and tuned out the flight attendant. I'd heard it all before, and besides: What was the likelihood that I'd be using my seat cushion as a floatation device, or needing an oxygen mask from the ceiling, or having to find the nearest exit?

> *"No temptation has overtaken you except what is common to mankind. And God is faithful; he will not let you be tempted beyond what you can bear. But when you are tempted, he will also provide a way out so that you can endure it."*[1]

I think I've treated God's instructions to me the same way. Back in college, when I couldn't seem to break free from the temptations of sexual sin, I spent a lot of time rationalizing my behavior and tuning out His voice. While there are many reasons we may choose to do this, for me the primary reason was I didn't want to admit things were out of control. I never thought my life would crash and leave me wishing I'd been paying attention when the safety instructions had been announced through the speakers.

🍎 🍎 🍎

God communicates to us by His Spirit, and sometimes He does this through the Bible, through other people who follow Him, or through prayer. Tuning in to God gets me ready for the battle and helps me know where to find the exits when I need them.

Who I Really Am

This struggle against sin isn't one we can fight from up in the very last seat of the nosebleed rows. It's more like hand-to-hand combat, and I don't know about you, but I don't usually think of myself as much of a warrior. I'm 5'2" on a good day, and when I look in the mirror, *Warrior* doesn't come to mind.

God tells me that—in Jesus—I am more than a conqueror.[2] The promise is the same for you. Because God loves us so much, He's guaranteed that we can come out victorious every time.

One of my favorite Bible stories is the one about Gideon, whose people had been harassed and tormented by the Midianites. These foes had worn them down to the point that they'd taken to hiding in caves to avoid being seen. One day, while Gideon was *hiding in a cave*, an angel showed up and said to him, "The LORD is with you, mighty warrior."[3]

I wonder if Gideon looked behind him to see if the angel was talking to someone else. Or maybe Gideon pointed to himself and said, *"Me?"*

God says the same thing about me, regardless of what I think I see in the mirror. I'm a warrior, and more than a conqueror. And so are you.

It's Not Just You

In these stories, we've heard about the temptations of sexual sin and gossip. If you're thinking that since "your sin" wasn't mentioned specifically, you're all alone in your struggle, nothing could be further from the truth.

One of the Enemy's biggest lies is convincing us we're the only Christian in our church, study group, or on the planet, who struggles with temptation. We think we're the only one who struggles with this particular sin in this particular way, and so we feel isolated and inadequate and unworthy.

But not one of us is alone. "No temptation has overtaken you except what is common to mankind." In other words, there's nothing new under the sun.[4] Your sin is not unbeatable. Your temptation isn't too big for God. You aren't even close to being the only one tempted in that way. And—no matter what you may hear to the contrary—God has an exit strategy just for you.

NUDGE NINE: Fall in Love Again

TEMPTED—Identifying Soul-Robbing Traps

Sometimes it's hard to accept *grace*—even to imagine that it actually applies to me. Here's what's difficult to believe about God's forgiveness:

Here are insecurity traps that I sometimes fall into:

I'd like Jesus to help me with:

TESTED—Learning How to Break Free

What Research Confirms About Relationship vs. Religion:

Our faith in Jesus Christ is really about an intimate relationship, not impersonal doctrines and religious practices. And relationships need ongoing, consistent connections in order to grow.

These two statements are pretty much no-brainers, right? Yet every one of us gets amnesia from time to time. The folks we talked to admit they sometimes forget these truths—especially in the heat of a temptation battle.

It's essential that we relearn how to connect with God during our devotional times. For example, instead of mechanically reading prayers, seek to learn to express them from your heart. Instead of opening your Bible solely with an information-gathering mindset, learn to *engage* Scripture.

Look for *connection, relationship,* and *spiritual transformation.* As you receive passages of Scripture, "listen" intently to God's personal message to you; do it relationally rather than seeking only to learn more about Him cognitively. Above all, allow God's Word to become an instrument of His control rather than a tool you control to accomplish your own goals.

In other words, in every way: Fall in love with Jesus!

A Proven Path:

(1) Give up impersonal religious practices.
(2) Focus on an intimate love relationship with Jesus.

Here's how our hearts are put into motion:

"Love the Lord your God with all your heart and with all your soul and with all your mind and with all your strength. . . . Love your neighbor as yourself. There is no commandment greater than these."[5]

What Christ-Followers Are Telling Us:

The word *struggle* means to "fight against" and to "put forth effort in order not to give in to something." I've come to accept that it's an unavoidable fact of life and a sure sign that our faith is alive. After all, dead things don't struggle!

Here's a mistake I made in the past: I lived like the "walking dead": I was among those Christ-followers who are defeated by their sins. . . . Day after day, I would cross lines and accept my soul-robbing behaviors as a way of life. "I simply can't change," I'd convinced myself, and then I'd do one of two things: I'd find a way to excuse my sin or I'd duck and cover. If consequences can be avoided simply by keeping a few secrets, then I'd shut my mouth and put on a holy façade. Being honest with myself and with God has made the difference. Now I can focus on real relationship and give up phony faith.

TRUE—Charting a Path Toward Change

1. *RECEIVE God's Word.* Read or listen to John 15:1–17.
2. *REFLECT on verses 9–11.* Pull them apart sentence by sentence, seeking God's personal message to you. Invite His Spirit to speak.

As the Father has loved me, so have I loved you. Now remain in my love. If you keep my commands, you will remain in my love, just as I have kept my Father's commands and remain in his love. I have told you this so that my joy may be in you and that your joy may be complete.

What is God saying to you? After a moment of silence before Him, converse with Him (talk and listen) through prayer.

Begin with general thoughts and impressions. . . . .

- "Heavenly Father, here's what I feel when I read these verses":

- "Here's what's hard for me, God—what I don't understand":

Now relate these verses to your specific struggles:

- "Here's what John 15:1–17 is telling me about Christ's love":

- "With your help, Lord, here's the kind of radical love I want to express to you and to my neighbors":

3. *MEMORIZE John 15:12–13.* Repeat it to yourself as often as needed. Write it out on an index card and post it where you'll see it.

My command is this: Love each other as I have loved you. Greater love has no one than this: to lay down one's life for one's friends.

4. *LISTEN to a friend.* Francis Chan says, about falling in love:

We know that God loves us and that we should love God. But there is no way I would characterize most Christians or most churches by their love for God. People in love act much differently than people with a sense of obligation. People do crazy things for love. Love has a way of making even the most difficult tasks feel simple and joyful. It has a way of pushing us to act with complete abandon and devotion.[6]

5. **RESPOND to God's nudges.** Try this "radical love" exercise:

- First, read what the late Rich Mullins had to say about love, priorities, and how he served Jesus Christ:

Part of my motivation for moving out to the reservation, quite honestly, was that I had become very weary of twentieth-century American evangelical Christianity. I think it's okay. I don't have anything against it. I just don't think it's the whole picture. I think that putting yourself in the midst of a culture unlike the one you grew up in helps you to keep some sort of sense of balance in the way you view your faith, your life, and things going on around you.

I still believe what marks us as Christians is not our doctrine in terms of a doctrinal statement. What marks us as Christians is our love for people. And if you love people you respect them. No one was ever won into the kingdom through snobbery. We come to know Christ through love. I think you can profess the Apostles' Creed until Jesus returns, but if you don't love somebody, you never were a Christian.[7]

- Next, think of people God wants you to love: A cantankerous co-worker, a single parent at church, or the nameless people who beg for money on street corners, the broken, the addicted, the unlovely . . . the "scary" folks who wouldn't dare set foot in church.

- Then ask God: *What must I do? How can I be your hands and feet—your face—to those I encounter? How can I love them?*

6. **PRAY.** Consider expressing this prayer by Dimitri of Rostov:

Come, our Light, and illumine our darkness.
Come, our Life, and raise us from death.

Come, our Physician, and heal our wounds.
Come, Flame of Divine Love, and burn up our sins.
Come, our King, sit upon the throne of our hearts
  and reign there.
For you alone are my King and my Lord.[8]

10

Unmasking the REAL Me

*Why Most of Us Are Afraid to Get Help . . .
and How We Can Change That Too*

"I feel so pitiful when I read the Bible," I (Cheryl) say to my husband.

"I know the feeling."

"Does everybody feel this way? Or am I just not *getting* it? How do I know?"

"Trust Jesus," he says—and I can't tell if he ends it with a period or a question mark.

I can't help but hear it the way I feel it. And there's the rub. Because I do trust Jesus—for you. I believe He loves you and watches over you and would go to the ends of the earth, for you.

But it's so much harder to trust Him for me. I must admit I do not enter into prayer with high expectations. I tend to feel that His answers for me will fall a little short of *yes*. That the resolution I need slips away right at the last moment. What am I to do with that? Am I just a faithless person disguising myself as a Christian?

I wish I knew if other people felt the same way. Yet I dare not ask out of the fear that I'm the only one. So I don't tell a soul.

When I was little, I used to wake in the morning to the sounds of Christian music coming from the TV in my parents' room across the hall. I would crawl out from underneath my bunched-up bed-spread, which by now was usually half on the floor. I'd slide my bare feet across the cool Formica tiles and onto the orange rug between my sister's bed and mine.

I remember like it was yesterday. I don't know where my mom found that rug. It was shaped like the fancy animal skin some people in Michigan lay in front of their cabin's fireplace "up north." But mine was *orange*. Originally, it might well have been dipped in "permanent Kool-Aid" and then hung out in the sun to dry. I loved it. I'd traverse it and go over to my parents' room.

Every Sunday morning (as I remember it) my dad would be there, shining his shoes for church. There'd be newspapers spread out at the end of the double bed to keep the polish from getting on the covers. He'd press a damp rag into the smoothness of brown, black, or cordovan polish in the little tin can with the *Kiwi* label. He seemed satisfied as he brushed the dark paste into a shine so bright he could almost see his reflection. Today, the smell of Kiwi polish still takes me back to those sweet and simple childhood mornings.

And I had my favorite Sunday morning rituals too. I was always excited to wear my black patent leather Mary Janes and tights. The latter always took a beating—I was lucky to get through a Sunday without ripping a new hole in one of the knees. But my mother was a pro with a needle and thread and always was able to repair them before the next weekend.

I can remember sitting in the back seat of the family car, running my finger along the ridge of gathered cotton and polyester.

The stitching would always leave an impression on my knee after I'd played on the fellowship hall floor while the grown-ups drank punch and ate cookies. But I knew that my mom was taking care of me and my bare kneecaps. It never entered my mind that I should try to cover up that row of stitches. I was just a little girl, living in a house where everybody loved me, and all I really had to hide, back then, was the scraped-up knee in my tights till we got back home.

❀ ❀ ❀

Then I grew up. I found myself in a new town and starting to attend a new church. My early Sunday excitement had been replaced with panic attacks. I'd sit on the edge of my bed, trying to remember how to catch my breath, willing myself to get up and just start moving. It was such a far cry from mornings with my dad and the polish and the tights with the knee hole.

But between those Sunday mornings as a little girl and these grown-up ones, I'd done a lot of living, and I'd experienced what I thought of as more than my fair share of disappointments and hurts with the people at church. I needed tremendous energy to pull myself together and make it through a grown-up Sunday morning. I'd slip into the back row of the sanctuary and try to disappear into the stained-glass windows while I searched the crowd for someone who could help me. Each week I left feeling empty and isolated, and glad Sunday morning was over so I could get out of there and be safe.

❀ ❀ ❀

I once attended a church where there were two other women. Of course, there were many others, but these two and I were friends. Until we weren't.

One day, one started giving me the cold shoulder—she avoided me in the sanctuary and stopped saving me a seat at the table in the fellowship hall.

So I asked her about it. I asked if I'd done something to offend her. We cried together and hugged and she said we were good.

But we weren't. And she continued to ignore me.

Shortly after that, the other woman started shutting me out too. So I called her and we set up a time to meet for lunch. As we sat in the downtown restaurant, she told me our friendship was over. She actually broke up with me. When I asked her why, she blamed it on God. She said she believed sometimes He brings people into our lives for a season, and the season for us was done.

We continued going to that same church—the two other women and me. But they wouldn't talk to me, or sit with me, or acknowledge me in any way.

Is Church a Hospital, or a Country Club?

If you've been part of a local church for any length of time, you have your own stories to tell. Maybe some of the unhappy ones sound a lot like these. When believers without a church are asked why they stopped attending, often they say something like this: "Church people are hypocrites. They say we're to love everyone, but then they pick and choose who to love."

I've witnessed some profoundly unforgiving and judgmental behavior in churches. I once heard someone say, "Church people will cut your throat so clean you won't know they've done it till you try to turn your head and it falls off." No wonder the idea of going to a new church—or even going to their own—is enough to give some people panic attacks.

Whether they meet in a rented movie theater, a towering cathedral, or a contemporary building with comfy seats that have cup holders for lattes, many churches call their center of worship a *sanctuary*. The word means a holy place of refuge. So why is it that so many of us don't turn to our own community of believers for support during difficult times? Why do we hide our struggles with fear, guilt, and depression, silently searching for help outside the church? Why are we terrified of being judged, brushed off, or turned away with a pat on the shoulder?

It's disappointing to learn that the place where we gather to worship God can sometimes be anything but a sanctuary. After we've been burned, the road to reopening our heart can be long and winding. We must reestablish mutual trust before we'll step forward and show our true selves. But many people have been so scarred, they worry that if their struggles became public knowledge they could be banished from the church altogether.

We show up with pasted-on smiles, frenetically shaking hands and going no deeper than "Good to see you" or "God bless you" when we encounter opportunities to connect with others. On the inside we're desperately hoping our anxiety and brokenness and addiction doesn't "show." Needle and thread certainly won't keep concealing all the stuff we're trying to cover up.

We are all looking for answers to our questions, help with our struggles, and support in the midst of our pain. However, by doggedly avoiding risk and any other "bad things" we imagine lie just behind the next greeting, we also avoid love and all the other possible "good things" as well.

What Christian Community Is Meant to Be

Luke gives us this beautiful depiction of the first-century church:

> All the believers were together and had everything in common. They sold property and possessions to give to anyone who had need. Every day they continued to meet together in the temple courts. They broke bread in their homes and ate together with glad and sincere hearts, praising God and enjoying the favor of

all the people. And the Lord added to their number daily those who were being saved.[1]

Doesn't that sound dreamy? It is a lovely vision of how we'd all like to experience church, and it seems so fantastic that sometimes I wonder if Luke was making things up.

Maybe you read this passage and think, *Yeah, right.* Or maybe, *That was then—things are so different now.* But the reality is that this is an accurate depiction of daily life in the early church. And there's a good chance this passage is included in God's Word to serve as a snapshot of how He intended us to live.

So what did these early Christians have that we can cultivate today? How were they able to forge a community where people could safely share their needs and have those needs met, right then and there?

Here are three factors that haven't changed across the centuries.

Church *Means "a Believing Community Coming Together"*

Sometimes it seems so much easier to skip church or not show up for our small group. It's easier to avoid situations where we might be asked how things are really going. If you gather the courage to go, maybe you remain quiet, praying no one asks you to share what's happening in your life.

But God intended us to be *together.* Sometimes we do step on each other, and sometimes we deliver or receive an elbow to the rib. That's life, here and now, because not one of us has become perfect. If we can stick it out and be part of the solution, we're likely to experience the true community we seek.

Church *Means "Sharing and Meeting Needs"*

At some point, everyone needs something. If you wait long enough, someday the person with the need will be the person with the ability to meet the need. One of the things we do is categorize others based on what they need. We make a quick assessment and decide he or she is lazy or thoughtless, sick or tired, sick *and* tired, or weird or needy or crazy or—worst of all—*sinful*. And who wants to be on the "receiving" end of that?

We're *all* needy. And we're all sinners. That's the reason Jesus came in the first place. At the bottom of every spoken need is an unspoken need for Jesus to show up. Amazingly, He has chosen *us* to be the way He does it.

Church *Means "Celebrating Our Faith in Jesus"*

When I read that passage in the second chapter of Acts, I get the sense that the early Christians knew how to throw a party. Sure there was time for being serious. The epistles are filled with practical advice about how we're to live in these years between when Jesus was raised and when He returns. But here, in these verses, we get a glimpse of the church with her shoes kicked off and her feet on the coffee table.

We need more such scenes. We need more joyful expectation, more carefree celebration, more shouts of *Hallelujah!* and more quiet whispers of praise. Simply put, truly glad hearts pave the way for broken hearts to experience safety and find healing.

Because of their joy, the early church had a good reputation. People with hurts, people with needs, and people at the end of their rope showed up on the doorstep because the church was a safe place. With them it was safe to take off ill-fitting masks with pasted-on smiles.

God did not intend for us to have to fake it in church, or *as* the church. He means for us to live our lives wide open with each other—our faults and struggles mixed in with support and compassion for one another.

🍎   🍎   🍎

We've been going together for six weeks now. She picks me up in her minivan and we go across town to the church with the organ and the choir and the ministers in long white robes. Sometimes we share dinner first, and across the table we talk about our families, or our work, or our children. Sometimes we just make the drive and chat as lights turn green, then yellow, then red.

On the sixth week, she drives me home and we sit in my driveway and talk about the tender places where we sometimes doubt, sometimes struggle, sometimes wonder if we even believe at all.

"I trust Jesus," I hear myself saying, and my words catch me by surprise. This isn't something I ever thought I'd say to anyone else. But I can't stop, and somewhere in there I realize I'm sharing and listening without a mask.

"I trust Jesus. For you. I believe Jesus loves you and that Jesus watches over you and that Jesus would go to the ends of the Earth. For you.

"But when I pray prayers to Jesus for myself, I'm fully expecting the answer to be just this side of *no*."

She rests her hand on the wheel and looks out through the windshield. Lightning doesn't strike. She doesn't seem at all surprised by words that sound to me like the thoughts of a faithless person disguised as a Christian.

And as I close the minivan door and walk up to my house, I can feel the wind on my face.

NUDGE TEN: Rethink Church

TEMPTED—Identifying Soul-Robbing Traps

I've had good and bad experiences at my church. I would describe my congregation as:

_____

_____

I would/would not share my struggles with friends at church because:

_____

_____

I'd like Jesus to help me with:

_____

_____

_____

_____

TESTED—Learning How to Break Free

What Research Confirms About Our Need for Community:

For decades the church has driven sinners away instead of embracing them. Said the late David Wilkerson:

> We stigmatize people with life-controlling problems. We take away their character by thinking of them as hopelessly hooked. We are so offended by their practices, we have made their sins so scandalous, we turn them into outcasts with no hope of return. We help to destroy their hunger for God by bringing down on them an avalanche of reproach and unforgiving wrath.[2]

Here are three problems we all must confront: We often take struggles underground because

(1) we're afraid of being scorned,
(2) we're convinced we'll never measure up to what God's Word says about purity and holiness, and
(3) we're clueless about how to practically, personally resist temptation.

A Proven Path:

(1) Stop masking weakness.
(2) Engage in (or help build) a safe community that promotes healing.

The first step is to come clean with our own sin. The second is to "carry each other's burdens."[3] Imagine how this kind of community would actually look! It would be a haven, a harbor where people could be real with one another and start to experience emotional and spiritual healing. This can be a reality for the church, but it begins with each one of us. So take the first step and set the example. *Rethink church!*

What Christ-Followers Are Telling Us:

Mix Scripture with the encouragement of believers who gently nudge but don't judge, and you've got a powerful way of breaking free from Satan's attacks. That's what I'm experiencing in a small group at my church. I struggle with an addiction to porn, and so do the other guys in my group. We know we have to overcome our sins . . . we know our relationship with Jesus can be so much better. And that's what we're helping each other find—real, transformational relationship with our Savior.

The most important thing for those of us here at my church is to learn to be real. I believe the biggest barrier to true Christianity is our false fronts. "I cannot change until I can admit what needs to be changed."

I smoke, I drink, and I don't fit a church's image of how a Christ-follower is to look and act. Yet I've given my life to Jesus and desperately want to know Him better. I even want to change. I just don't know how. I really need the support of other believers instead of constant judgment and condemnation. I recently found a Christian outreach for people like me, and it's starting to help. We have Bible studies together and pray for each other. We even share meals. We're not really a formal church—we meet in an abandoned storefront—but this is starting to feel like family to me . . . which is what I think church should be.

With the vast differences between Catholics, Baptists, Presbyterians, non-denominationalists, etc., I've found it hard to discern the actual message of the Bible. Here's what I'm starting to learn: I must focus on God's Word—what He's saying to *me*—and not get caught up in "factions." That's key to growth.

TRUE—Charting a Path Toward Change

1. RECEIVE God's Word. Read or listen to Ephesians 2:11–22.

2. REFLECT on verses 19–22. Pull them apart sentence by sentence, seeking God's personal message to you. Invite His Spirit to speak.

You are no longer foreigners and strangers, but fellow citizens with God's people and also members of his household, built on the foundation of the apostles and prophets, with Christ Jesus himself as the chief cornerstone. In him the whole building is joined together and rises to become a holy temple in the Lord. And in him you too are being built together to become a dwelling in which God lives by his Spirit.

What is God saying to you? After a moment of silence before Him, converse with Him (talk and listen) through prayer.

Begin with general thoughts and impressions:

- "Heavenly Father, here's what I feel when I read these verses":

_____

_____

- "Here's what's hard for me, God—what I don't understand":

_____

_____

Now relate these verses to your specific struggles:

- "Here's what Ephesians 2:11–22 is telling me about your church and the important part I have in it":

_____

_____

- "With your help, Lord, here's how I'll endeavor to rethink church and reconnect with it":

_____

_____

3. *MEMORIZE Ephesians 2:13–14.* Repeat it to yourself as often as needed. Write it out on an index card and post it where you'll see it.

> In Christ Jesus you who once were far away have been brought near by the blood of Christ. For he himself is our peace, who has made the two groups one and has destroyed the barrier, the dividing wall of hostility.

4. *LISTEN to a friend.* Madeleine L'Engle says, about the importance of restored relationships within the church body:

> If the Lord's table is the prototype of the family table, then, if I think in terms of the family table, I know that I cannot sit down to bread and wine until I've said I'm sorry, until reparations have been made, relations restored. When one of our children had done something particularly unworthy, if it had come out into the open before dinner, if there had been an "I'm sorry," and there had been acceptance, and love, then would follow the happiest dinner possible, full of laughter and fun. If there was something still hidden; if one child, or as sometimes happens, one parent, was out of joint with the family and the world, that would destroy the atmosphere of the whole meal.[4]

5. *RESPOND to God's nudges.* Try this "Community Connection" exercise:

- *Evaluate your church experience.* Before I (Mike) became a Christian, one of my biggest stumbling blocks was the hypocrisy I saw in certain so-called "followers of Christ." At times I couldn't help feeling that church was just a building full of angry finger-pointers. Where was the hope? Where was the unity? Then I met a guy, Scott, who actually lived his faith. Scott was real—strong in his convictions, yet he didn't try to hide his weaknesses. I never felt judged by him. In fact, the more time we spent, the more I began to sense Christ's presence. My friend even led me in prayer the day

I committed my life to Jesus. I'll always remember one of his first pieces of advice: "Get your eyes off other Christians because they'll sometimes let you down. Even I'll disappoint you. Instead, focus on Jesus. Trust Him, follow Him, and do all you can to be like Him." So instead of getting angry or giving up, I decided to look for the "Scotts" in my church and seek to reflect the face of Christ.

Who are the "Scotts" in your church?

_____

_____

In what ways can you be a "Scott" to others?

_____

_____

- *Evaluate your own hypocrisy.* As David Wilkerson pointed out, we tend to bring others down with us:

If you rob a sinner of his character, if you take away his dignity, if you focus only on his failures, if you treat him as a nonperson, if you shut off all his roads of retreat—he is driven to hardness. He becomes calloused and begins to fight back because that is all that is left for him. It is an easy step from hardness to violence. Humiliate the sinner, take away his sense of worth, and soon you will have driven him to total remorse. If there is no God in him to support him, he will lose all hope and finally give himself over to those who will accept him. Then he often uses that hostility as an excuse to remain in his sin.[5]

What frustrates you about church?

_____

_____

What can you change?

- *Evaluate your service to others.* Here's what Mother Teresa said about carrying one another's burdens:

We all long for heaven where God is, but we have it in our power to be in heaven with Him right now—to be happy with Him at this very moment. But being happy with Him now means loving like He loves, helping like He helps, giving as He gives, serving as He serves, rescuing as He rescues, being with Him twenty-four hours a day—touching Him in His distressing disguise.

How does caring for others help you with your own sin battle?

6. PRAY. Consider expressing this prayer by Janet Lees:

God of good ideas, who began the world with light and word, who began again with flood and rainbow; we acknowledge our frustration with your church: its committees and structures, its methods and systems. These things have made us angry and sapped our energy.

God of new beginnings, who began a new way of living with resurrection, who began a new community with tongues of fire; begin again here that structures may bend like dancing saplings; that past, present, and future may be woven into a fresh path of commitment.

May our ideas for your world and this community resonate in your presence, so that tested, tried, and challenged they may blossom in us as do dry places when longed-for rain falls.[6]

Ending Point

Giving Grace Another Chance

When I (Michelle) was in elementary school, I stole a necklace right out of my classmate's open desk. As she bent over a sheet of math problems, I reached my hand around her back and into her desk, slowly pulled out the glittering treasure, and stuffed it into my pants pocket.

The moment I saw the dazzling faux sapphire on the black velvet strand, I coveted it. I didn't care that it wasn't mine. I didn't think about the fact that taking it would be stealing; I simply *wanted* it. And so without considering the consequences, I took it.

The instant that necklace was balled up in my pocket, I regretted it. I knew what I'd done was wrong, and worse, I knew I'd committed a sin, a bad sin, one of the worst kinds. I'd broken one of the Ten Commandments.

I also knew that if I failed to confess my sin to a priest, eventually I'd end up in hell. Forever.

The problem was, I was afraid to confess.

Every couple of weeks or so, I'd steel myself outside the confessional's red velvet curtain. Then I'd take a deep breath, duck inside, and crouch on the plush kneeler. But when the window slid open and the priest's quiet voice on the other side urged, "You may begin, my child," I'd freeze. I'd rattle off my standard sin list—disobeying my parents, antagonizing my sister, telling white lies—but I'd always swallow any mention of "the big one." With the sin of stealing lodged in my throat, I'd push back the curtain and step out, kneel in the pew to recite my penance, and berate myself for my cowardice.

*   *   *

After I stole the necklace, I always approached Lent—which I viewed as a window of self-inflicted punishment—with mixed dread and anticipation. Part of me hoped that if I gave up enough chocolate, gagged back enough broiled scrod on Fridays, and did enough "good deeds" for others, I somehow could make up for my one huge unconfessed sin. In other words, I hoped I could even the scales. I saw Lent as a time of atonement, but atonement tinged with despair, because I knew I could never succeed. I knew I couldn't truly win back God's love. While I sheepishly wiped the ash cross on my forehead, creating a black smudge, I knew I wasn't able to wipe away my sins so easily.

I never considered giving the necklace back to its owner because I was too ashamed and too afraid of the punishment. And truthfully, I'm not sure I wanted to give it back. Even though I could never wear it anywhere but behind the tightly closed door of my bedroom, I still loved that necklace. I was proud of it, proud that I owned it. Furthermore, I was too proud to tarnish my reputation by giving it back and admitting my wrongdoing.

*   *   *

I lived with the theft hanging over my head for years, convinced and terrified that I'd burn in hell, yet even more terrified to confess the sin. After all, I was a good girl—I got good grades, delivered newspapers after school to earn a few dollars each week, visited my elderly great aunt in the nursing home without complaint. I wasn't the type who stole. That kind of sin was too evil, and it was committed by "other people," very bad people.

Stealing the necklace at age seven was the beginning of the end of faith for me. After that day, I wasn't able to have anything more than a contrived connection with God, because the sin stood between us. Deep in my heart, I was convinced my sin was too terrible to confess, too terrible to be forgiven. I was too far gone to be helped. And so for more than two decades, I had a pretend relationship with God—which is to say, no relationship at all.

Enter Grace

For my first thirty-five or so years, I didn't understand the concept of grace. I simply didn't get it. The word itself wasn't a big part of my childhood religion. As a kid squirming in the worn wooden pew, I heard a lot about sin, death, hell, punishment, repentance, and the devil from the pulpit, but I don't recall ever hearing about grace. As far as I knew, grace was what we uttered once a year before ladling gravy over turkey and mashed potatoes. In my mind, *grace* was a fancy word for a "thank-you prayer."

It wasn't until I began to attend church with my husband that I began to "get" grace. And it was a steep learning curve. One morning I turned to Brad outside as we walked to the car after the service. "What's all this about love and grace?" I asked, stopping on the gravel to face him. "That's all they seem to talk about here—love and grace, love and grace. I don't get it." I could understand so little about it, grace didn't fit with my view of reality.

Reading the parable of the vineyard workers[1] confused me further. Maybe you're familiar with the gist of the story, which goes like this:

A landowner hires a group of workers in the early morning to labor in his vineyard all day for payment of one denarius. Later in the morning, he hires another group, and then he hires more laborers three more times during the day: at noon, 3:00 p.m., and 5:00 p.m.

When evening comes, the landowner instructs his supervisor to pay all the workers their denarius, beginning with the group hired at five in the afternoon and ending with the workers hired first. Not surprisingly, the workers who toiled for twelve hours are furious and resentful that their pay equals that of the workers who labored for only an hour.

The first few times I read this parable I thought, *What a complete rip-off!* I related to the disgruntled workers who slaved in the heat all day for the same pay as those who got off easy and sauntered in for sixty minutes at day's end. I could not fathom why in the world a boss would be foolish enough to pay the same wages for top-notch, tireless work as for work of convenience, done on its own terms. In my equal-pay-for-equal-work world, and according to my corporate-ladder work ethic, this made zero sense.

Furthermore, I couldn't grasp the owner's response to the bitter workers:

I am not being unfair to you, friend. Didn't you agree to work for a denarius? Take your pay and go. I want to give the one who was hired last the same as I gave you. Don't I have the right to do what I want with my own money? Or are you envious because I am generous?[2]

All I could think when I read that was, "No! This isn't generosity! This is bad business—sheer stupidity!"

It took me a long time to realize this story is not about stupidity. It's about grace.

It's true that this story doesn't make a bit of fiscal or managerial sense. But that's the whole point. *Grace* doesn't make sense; it's not *supposed* to make sense. Grace cannot be calculated or formulated. Grace cannot be earned, and it's not a reward for a job well done. Grace is a gift—free and undeserved. Grace obliterates all the rules.

We all get grace, each and every one of us, the first as well as the last. The question is: *Will we accept it?*

Accepting an Undeserved Gift

An experience at work recently brought the notion of grace to life for me in a very practical way. It began with a voicemail message from Cathy in Human Resources: "Michelle! I pulled your name in the drawing for a pizza gift card! Stop by my office to pick it up when you have a chance."

Me? I won something? That never happens! I bounded up the stairs two at a time.

"Hey! I heard I won a gift card . . . what was the drawing for?" I asked as I leaned against her doorframe, my hand outstretched to accept the gift.

Turns out, I didn't deserve it. You see, my name was drawn from a pool of more than a hundred employees who'd submitted their United Way workplace campaign contribution cards. I'd dutifully completed it as requested and turned it in to HR, but I hadn't contributed a dime. On the donation line, I'd penciled in a big, fat zero.

"I don't think I can accept this," I admitted sheepishly to Cathy, holding out the card. "Um, I sort of didn't contribute anything, so I don't think I should take the gift card. Maybe you should pick someone who actually donated to the campaign."

ٰ   ٰ   ٰ

In the end, Cathy insisted I take the gift. I'd submitted the required campaign materials, and that was enough for her. Plus, she was probably too mortified to snatch it back, since she'd already placed the card in my open palm. So I slunk out of her office with the $10 gift in my hand.

The more I thought about this awkward situation, the more it reminded me of grace. After all, grace is a free gift—the be-all and end-all of free gifts. None of us deserves God's love and forgiveness. None of us deserves eternal salvation, a free ticket to heaven.

We may *think* we deserve it, telling ourselves we've worked hard and "been good," but the truth is, "I deserve" doesn't enter into the grace equation. We don't earn grace, we don't sacrifice for it, and we don't work to get it.

Likewise, even if we conclude we *don't* deserve grace on account of our bad behavior or persistent failings, we are still granted it. Grace isn't withheld from us just because we haven't met a certain standard.

Grace depends entirely on one factor: The ultimate sacrifice of Jesus. His death on the cross—the giving of His own life for each one of us—guarantees that we're forgiven again and again, loved abundantly, always, and given eternal life. Forgiveness, love, and salvation are God's great gift card.

Two Steps Forward, One Step Back

Even though I understand the concept of grace in my head a bit better these days, from time to time I still forget what it means for me personally.

There are the crabby days, the snap-at-my-husband days, the gossipy days, the yell-at-the-kids (again) days. Days when I beat myself up for being a bad wife, bad mother, bad housekeeper, bad employee, bad Christian. Days when I easily convince myself that grace is for others but certainly not for me.

Let me share an example. A couple of years ago, after a particularly inspiring sermon, I decided I'd aspire to exude grace and peace throughout my day, every day, and to whoever crossed my path. The first few hours were a snap. I was patient and cheery, loving and kind. Grace and peace oozed from my every pore . . . for four straight hours. The trouble is, a day is long—and frankly, who can exude grace and peace for *sixteen* consecutive hours?

As it turns out, the vacuum cleaner broke me. As I pushed the floor brush along the baseboard and beneath the couch, my brand-new vacuum suddenly lost all suction. I switched it off, peered into the hose, tapped the attachment on the floor, and then switched it back on. Still nothing. The kids, glimpsing my wild look, scurried like mice to their rooms as I heaved attachments and hoses onto the couch, slammed the dirty canister over the garbage can, and stomped back into the living room, muttering furiously under my breath.

"Don't even bother," I fumed to Brad, as he patiently detached the hose. "What a complete waste. It's totally broken—ruined. What a piece of junk. I can't believe this."

I ranted and raved in full tantrum mode as he shined a flashlight into the hose, poked and prodded with a pencil, and fished out a motley mass of hair, string, tree needles, and an acorn. Then he snapped the canister and hose back into place and switched the thing on. It purred sweetly, full suction restored.

Suffice to say, I did not spread grace and peace throughout my home that Saturday. I hadn't even made it through a day with my intentions and aspirations intact. I was disappointed and disgusted with myself. And I was embarrassed, seeing as I'd announced my plan to my family in a grand proclamation that very morning, yet hadn't gotten through five hours before disintegrating into a raving lunatic.

What I learned, though, with that failed grace-and-peace project, is that good intentions aren't enough. We will fail, over and over again, despite our strongest resolve and our best-laid plans. We are flawed. We are fallible. We make mistakes. A few of us heave vacuum parts around the living room. Although Jesus asks us to be perfect, we cannot achieve perfection because we are simply not Him.

Maybe this is hard for you, this knowledge that you'll fall short. I know it is for me. As a Type-A overachiever I don't like to fail. I set the bar high, and I'm hard on myself when I don't clear it. The key, though, is that God knows this about me, just like He knows all the quirks that make you uniquely *you*. And He loves us—every part of us—no matter what.

Because of that love, I keep trying, knowing I'll stray, knowing I'll flounder and fail, but also confident I'll survive, thrive, and ultimately, with His grace, become a better, humbler, more patient, slightly more Jesus-like person. On some days. And on the days I fail, well, I'll just start over again.

After all, that's what grace is, right? It's the ultimate do-over, the infinite second chance. God gives us another chance, and another and another. Day in and day out. He works with us and through us. And He never gives up on us.

Grace Is for Everyone

Because I'm so hard on myself, sometimes I think that gives me free rein to be critical of others too. For example, I realized recently that I classify sins. I consider some far worse than others, and the people who commit *those* sins worse off than me.

This is where the prophet Jonah went astray: He couldn't comprehend and accept the fact that the Ninevites, a wicked and evil people, could be offered the same grace he was. "I'm so angry, I wish I were dead," Jonah tells God, when he learns that God will show compassion to those Assyrians.[3]

Jonah considers their sins unforgivable. Despite the fact that he has been given a second chance also, he's still blind to the concept of grace. He considers "Ninevite sin" much worse than his own, and essentially says to God, "It's not fair that you're not going to send disaster upon them!"[4]

I admit, I have my Jonah moments, and maybe you do too. I wonder sometimes how a sin like murder or theft can be forgiven in the same way as some other sins. There was a time, not all that long ago, that I simply didn't get the point of prison ministry. I couldn't understand why murderers, rapists, child molesters, and other "such" criminals deserved spiritual ministration. I believed others deserved spiritual attention more than those behind bars, simply because "those people" had brought misfortune upon themselves and wreaked havoc on the lives of others.

I classified sins into a hierarchy of bland, bad, and unforgivable, and I embraced this system largely because I assumed it let me off the hook (disregarding the fact that I broke one of the Ten Commandments, of course!).

I had a whole hierarchy worked out, and I figured if I stayed ahead of most of the sinners on the bottom rungs, then hey, I was doing okay, right?

My formula seemed to work pretty well, until I read Romans 3:23: *"All have sinned and fall short of the glory of God."*

Notice how it doesn't say, "The murderer falls harder," or "The rapist falls farther." We're all lumped together as sinners. And we all fall short.

This means that if the murderer repents of his sin, he gets the same grace I get for repenting that I yelled at my kids this morning. Part of me protests, "No fair! How can *he* get the same grace

Accepting Grace in the Everyday

The promise that grace is for everyone sounds great on paper. But how do you come to truly believe it in your heart? Here are some concrete steps that may help to deepen your understanding of grace.

- *Read:* The Bible talks a lot about grace; here are some passages that tackle the subject head on and may lead you to fuller understanding: Romans 3:9–26; Matthew 20:1–16; Ephesians 2:2–10.

- *Pray:* Sometimes we forget to ask God for help when we're struggling. If you have trouble believing God unconditionally loves and forgives you, pray this prayer every day until you begin to feel its truth seep into your heart: *Lord, please open my heart to your love, so that I may truly grow to know you as the God who always loves, accepts, and forgives me, no matter what. Amen.*

- *Reflect:* Think for a moment about a time when you forgave someone you loved—perhaps your child, spouse, sibling, or close friend—or when a loved one forgave you for a wrong. Ponder the human heart's capacity for love, even through challenging circumstances, and know that God's capacity to love is infinitely greater.

- *Converse:* Sometimes it's helpful to talk through questions and doubts with a trusted confidant—a minister, priest, friend, family member, or counselor. Perhaps you're holding on to guilt from a recent or past transgression. Unburdening yourself of this weight may help you open yourself up more fully to accept God's love and forgiveness.

- *Watch:* See the film *Amazing Grace*, a true story that recounts John Newton's experiences as a slave ship crewman and subsequent conversion in the late 1770s, which inspired him to write the poem later used as the lyrics to the hymn.

as *me*? Shouldn't it be at least a *little* less?" But that's the whole point: Grace isn't fair because none of us, no matter how egregious or inconsequential we consider our sins, deserves grace. The gift is that we get grace anyway.

Jesus explains it like this in the Sermon on the Mount:

You have heard that it was said to the people long ago, "You shall not murder, and anyone who murders will be subject to judgment." But I tell you that anyone who is angry with a brother or sister will be subject to judgment.[5]

Turns out, Jesus doesn't classify sins into a hierarchy. In His eyes, we're all equally broken. In sinning, we turn from God. It doesn't matter whether we turn away a little bit or a lot; it's the act of turning away that matters.

While it may make me feel better to point a finger at someone whose sins I deem worse than mine, we're all broken. On some days I'll be (or seem) more broken than you; on some days you'll be (or seem) more broken than me. It matters little, really, who is, or appears, more or less broken. In the end, broken is broken.

And God extends His grace to everyone, always, and equally— both to those broken just a bit and to those broken to bits.

Appendix

Calvin, Luther, and Arminius

Three Protestant Views About Sin and Salvation

Is it true that "once saved, [we're] always saved," or can Christ-followers actually lose their salvation? And did God choose some for eternal life, but not others?

If "God's elect" *are* predestined for eternal life, doesn't that give them a kind of license to sin during their short stay on earth? Aren't they bound for heaven anyway?

On the other hand . . .

Because sin separates us from God, and since the New Testament says that all who place hope in Christ "purify themselves, just as he is pure,"[1] could it be that unholy living isn't even an option for the Lord's people? In other words, Jesus destroyed the "sin license" and gives those who follow Him a new desire (essentially, a brand-new heart) that enables them to be righteous, "just as he is righteous."[2]

Good stuff to think about.

In fact, these matters have been pondered, dissected, and debated for eons. And should you ever poke your head into a postgraduate theology class, you'll probably encounter a bunch of other such lofty-seeming concepts as well:

- Should we subscribe to monergism or synergism?
- When it comes to human will, do we embrace "total depravity without free will because of God's sovereignty," or does depravity not prevent free will?
- Is unconditional election biblically sound, or is election conditional?
- How should we view God's grace? For instance, as prevenient? How about as irresistible?
- Exactly what was accomplished on the cross—limited atonement, or justification for all who believe completed at Christ's death; the possibility of justification for all who believe but completed only upon choosing faith in Jesus?
- Do believers have an assurance of preservation, or is there a possibility of final apostasy?

"Moner-syner-limited-but-irresistible" . . . WHAT?!

Isn't this all just theobabble? The pursuit of religiosity? Distractions from what really matters: knowing, trusting, and following Jesus Christ?

No, because doctrine matters. Firming up our faith and cluing in to the whys behind our beliefs can help us to live Christ, overcome the things that trip us up, and ultimately know Him better—which makes all the difference in the world.

On the other hand, wasting energy debating the "gray areas" of faith (and human traditions) can be distractions. In C. S. Lewis's words:

If I may trust my personal experience, no doctrine is, for the moment, dimmer to the eye of faith than that which a man has just successfully defended.[3]

Doctrines are not God: they are only a kind of map. But that map is based on the experience of hundreds of people who really were in touch with God.[4]

In these few pages, let's take a brief look at the views of three men who most definitely were in touch with God. Whether or not we realize it, much of what Protestants claim and proclaim about the Lord (that is, our doctrinal positions) has been influenced by their teachings.

John Calvin (1509–1564) was a French theologian, apologist, and pastor during the Protestant Reformation. He wrote the *Institutes of the Christian Religion* and many other works. His theology has influenced a variety of denominations, including Presbyterians, American Baptists, and Congregationalists.

Martin Luther (1483–1546) was a German priest, Bible translator, and theology professor during the Reformation. He wrote the *Large Catechism* (a manual for pastors and teachers), the *Small Catechism* (devotional material for congregants), and many other works. His theology has influenced a variety of denominations but most specifically the Lutheran church.

Jacobus (aka Jacob or James) Arminius (1560–1609) was a Dutch theologian, pastor, and professor of theology during the Reformation. He wrote extensively in objection to Calvinist tenets, and most of his arguments are presented in *The Complete Works of James Arminius*. His denominational influence includes many Methodist and Holiness churches and especially the Church of the Nazarene.

Do you know how your church lines up in terms of the theology of these men? How about you personally? Do you lean toward

Calvinism, Lutheranism, or Arminianism . . . or do you subscribe to an amalgamation of more than one view? Getting a handle on the issues can provide us with that trustworthy "map" Lewis mentions.

However, as we consider anyone's teachings, we must remind ourselves that believers are followers of Jesus Christ—not of Calvin, Luther, or Arminius. Just as they sought to do, we must draw our doctrines from God's Word and compare what we hear from others to what He says.

A Kansas City pastor beautifully sums up a universal doctrine we all should take to heart:

> A relationship in close communication with Jesus is the only way to live. As we abide in Him, He lives through us. [This relationship] is dynamic, real, and personal. It is an invitation to a holy "highway" of living. Jesus has an intimate relationship with the Father and intends for us to know that we can be one in and with Him. [This] is the great invitation to be a holy people, not in our efforts, abilities, or energies, but in a death to self so that He might live in us moment by moment. Without Him in this moment, nothing but darkness remains.[5]

Below is a chart that highlights some core beliefs about sin and salvation held by most Protestant churches. Please note: Countless volumes of books, and even entire seminaries, are devoted to such teachings. Stripping down complicated theology to sound bites has very intrinsic limits, and admittedly this presentation is woefully simplistic. Our goal is merely to tip our hat to the spectrum of viewpoints within Christianity and, hopefully, to make the pages of this book even more relevant to your own perspectives.

As you read or reread *Tempted, Tested, True,* use this material as a reference point. The first column includes a definition of a spiritual topic and applicable references. The subsequent columns indicate various doctrinal stances. (Do pay attention to the footnotes throughout. Some suggest websites and other helpful resources.)

Spiritual Issue	Calvinism	Lutheranism	Arminianism
Human Sinfulness: Transgression of God's will; lawlessness; original sin (all of humanity has inherited from Adam and Eve a corrupt nature). *A Biblical Foundation:* Genesis 3; Matthew 15:19; Romans 3:23; 5:12–21; 1 John 3:4	Every person born in this world is enslaved to sin and inclined to serve selfish interests. Spiritually, individuals lack free will and cannot choose to follow God without the Holy Spirit's influence. (Doctrine: Total Depravity.)[6]	Humankind is "saddled with original sin, born sinful and unable to avoid committing sinful acts."[7] Every human thought and deed is infected with sin and sinful motives. But after regeneration through Jesus Christ, a person possesses the will "to act in order to fulfill his good purpose."[8]	The human race was created in God's image and given the ability to choose between right and wrong. While Adam's fall resulted in sin and depravity, "the grace of God through Jesus Christ is freely bestowed upon all people, enabling all who will to turn from sin to righteousness."[9]
Divine Election: God, omniscient and sovereign, foreknew and predestined the course of human history and the lives of individuals. *A Biblical Foundation:* Isaiah 45:22; John 3:16; 15:16; Romans 8:29–30; Ephesians 1:4–5, 11; 1 Timothy 2:3–4; Revelation 22:17	Before creation God chose certain individuals for eternal salvation according to His own purposes, not their own choices or actions. Only the sins of the elect were atoned for by Christ's death on the cross.[10] (Doctrines: Unconditional Election and Particular Atonement [also consider meaning of predestination].)[11]	Due to humanity's fallen state, individual salvation is extended only by acts of God. People have free will as to civil righteousness but cannot work spiritual righteousness into their hearts without the Spirit's aid. "We reject also the Calvinistic perversion . . . that God does not desire to convert and save all hearers of the Word, but only a portion of them."[12]	Christ's death is for all of humanity. The sovereign God loves His creation, so He offers salvation to all who will believe, repent, and receive forgiveness. Yet humans, by free will, can choose to remain in sin and reject salvation. (Doctrine: Conditional Election [also consider meanings of free will and prevenient grace].)[13]

Spiritual Issue	Calvinism	Lutheranism	Arminianism
Conversion: God's call to become His children, heirs to eternal life; act of turnng to; being brought into right relationship with Christ. *A Biblical Foundation:* Jeremiah 1:5; Ezekiel 34:11; Matthew 4:18–22; 18:3; Luke 5:1–11; John 6:44;14:6; Acts 15:3; Titus 2:11	Coming to Christ in faith is by God's intervention, not human will. "It is not violent so as to compel [us] by external force; but still it is a powerful impulse of the Holy Spirit, which makes [us] willing who formerly were unwilling and reluctant."[14] (Doctrine: Irresistible Grace [see discussions about monergism vs. synergism also].)[15]	People resist God's Word and will until God wakens (from death in sin), enlightens, and renews.[16] Conversion is not taken out of God's hands and made to depend on what He does or leaves undone. We owe salvation solely to His grace. (Nonconversion is on the human account, though, by resisting the Spirit.[17] See discussions about *means of grace*.)[18]	God extends "prevenient" grace that precedes human decision, drawing a person toward salvation, which is equally provided to all and enables people to engage their God-given free will to choose or reject Him. (See discussions about prevenient grace and free will.)[19]
Apostasy: The act of falling away from God; backsliding. *A Biblical Foundation:* Deuteronomy 28:1–2; Ezekiel 18:1–4; John 5:24; Romans 8:1; 1 Corinthians 1:1–2; 15:24–28; Galatians 6:7–8; Ephesians 1:4–23; 2:1–10; 1 John 1:7–9; 3:3–10	A person who sincerely trusts Christ for salvation "will never fall away from the state of grace, but shall persevere to the end. Believers may fall into sin through neglect and temptation, whereby they grieve the Spirit . . . yet they shall be kept by the power of God through faith unto salvation."[20] (Doctrine: Perseverance of the Saints)	Falling away is possible. "When holy men, still having and feeling original sin, also daily repenting of and striving with it . . . fall into manifest sins . . . then faith and the Holy Ghost has departed from them [they cast out faith and the Holy Ghost]."[21] Yet God has promised to preserve, from beginning to end, the faith of true believers: "My sheep listen to my voice; I know them, and they follow me. I give them eternal life, and they shall never perish; no one will snatch them out of my hand."[22]	Believers who are being regenerated and sanctified by Christ can still "fall from grace and apostatize and, unless they repent of their sins, be hopelessly and eternally lost."[23]

Worksheet 1

My Spiritual Weakness Chart

Day	Time of Day	Place	Circumstances	Emotions
Monday				
Tuesday				
Wednesday				
Thursday				
Friday				
Saturday				
Sunday				

Worksheet 2

My Spiritual Interruptions Chart

How MY Heart Is "Interrupted" Throughout the Day

24-Hour Cycle	When Temptation Is Strongest	How I Feel	Specific Struggle	Spiritual Interruption
Early Morning (Night) 12–3				
Early Morning (Night) 3–6				
Early Morning 6–9				
Midmorning 9–12				
Noon Hour 12–1				
Early Afternoon 1–2				
Midafternoon 3–5				
Early Evening 5–7				
Midevening 7–9				
Late Evening 9–12				

Contributors

Theresa Cox, writer, church leader, and physician's assistant, contributed to chapter 2, specifically on the temptation cycle stages (based on James 1:13–15). Theresa lives in Colorado Springs with Clarence, an ornery (but huggable) cocker spaniel.

David Barshinger, PhD, writer, minister, instructor, and recent graduate of Trinity Evangelical Divinity School, lent expert insight on soul-robbing choices and on what the Bible teaches about the "Seven Deadly Sins" in chapter 3. David—"head-over-heels in love" with his wife and the proud daddy of three "amazing boys"—and his family live near Chicago.

Pamela Ovwigho, PhD, CBE's executive director, carried out much of the research that became this book's evidentiary foundation, and augmented chapters 4 and 5 with findings on the "most common temptations." When she's not asking people questions about their spiritual lives, Pam is busy fixing up the 100-year-old Nebraska farmhouse she shares with her husband and children.

Kelly Combs, wife, mom, writer, and speaker, supplied the story in chapter 6 of how she overcame a stolen childhood and emerged as a restored child of God. Her writing has been published in *Guideposts,* in Gary Chapman's *Love Is a Verb* devotional, and in many other venues. Kelly and her family live in Virginia.

Sue Cameron, wife, grandmother, writer, speaker, and blogger (aka "Grammy Sue"), helped in chapter 8 to illustrate how pornography affects married couples. Sue and her family live in Texas.

Deidra Riggs, freelance writer, speaker, small-event planner, managing editor of TheHighCalling.org, and blogger ("Jumping Tandem"), enhanced chapters 9 and 10 with stories of the healing that comes as we "unmask our true selves" to overcome struggle. Deidra and her husband have two adult children and one farm dog. They live in Lincoln, Nebraska.

Michelle DeRusha, writer and blogger ("Graceful"), shares a personal story in "Ending Point" that demonstrates how God loves us when we're broken just a bit and when we're broken to bits. Mom to two rambunctious, bug-loving boys—Noah and Rowan—and wife to Brad, Michelle worked in New York City as associate editor for *Art & Antiques* magazine. The DeRushas now live in Lincoln, Nebraska.

Notes

Starting Point: Immobilized and Neutralized

1. William Griffin, *Jesus for Children* (Minneapolis: Winston, 1985), 115–117. This story is based on the Great Commission (Matthew 28:16–20).

2. Peter Marshall, *Mr. Jones, Meet the Master* (Grand Rapids, MI: Revell, 1949), 177–178.

3. Luke 15:20–24 THE MESSAGE

4. See Rev. Dirk R. Buursma, Rev. Verlyn D. Verbrugge, and Jean Syswerda, eds., *Daylight Devotional Bible* (Grand Rapids, MI: Zondervan, 1988), 1109.

5. C. S. Lewis, *Mere Christianity* (San Francisco: HarperSanFrancisco, 2001), 3.11.

6. W. Jay Wood, "Three Faces of Greed: Another Vice That Looks Like a Virtue" at ChristianityToday.com, posted 01/07/05. christianitytoday.com/ct/2005/ January/27.34.html.

7. Scot McKnight, "Why Doesn't Anybody Talk About Sin?" at Relevant Magazine.com, posted 07/13/11. relevantmagazine.com/god/deeper-walk/features /26172-why-doesnt-anybody-talk-about-sin-anymore.

8. e.g., see Romans 3:21–31. Unless otherwise noted, all quoted Scripture in this book is from the *New International Version* (NIV2011).

9. Psalm 32:1–2 ESV

10. See Psalm 119:11.

11. Conducted by the Center for Bible Engagement, a division of Back to the Bible.

Chapter 1: From the Garden to the Desert . . . and On to the Cross

1. Anonymous

2. See Genesis 1.

3. Genesis 1:26 THE MESSAGE

4. Genesis 1:28 THE MESSAGE

5. See Genesis 1.

6. Genesis 2:15

7. Genesis 3:8

8. See Steven James, *Story: Recapture the Mystery* (Grand Rapids, MI: Revell, 2006), 20.

9. Ibid.

10. See Karen C. Hinckley and Karen Lee-Thorp, *The Story of Stories: The Bible in Narrative Form* (Colorado Springs: NavPress, 1991), 15.

11. Ibid.

12. Ibid.

13. See Genesis 2:17 THE MESSAGE

14. Genesis 3:4–5

15. See Hinckley and Lee-Thorp, *The Story of Stories,* 16–17.

16. McKnight, "Why Doesn't Anybody Talk About Sin?"

17. Proverbs 14:12

18. James, *Story,* 89.

19. See Genesis 5–9.

20. See Exodus 20.

21. See Hinckley and Lee-Thorp, *The Story of Stories,* 68.

22. See John Fischer, "On a Hill Too Far Away" in *Breakaway* (April 2006): 6–7.

23. Ibid., 6.

24. Ibid.

25. See Matthew 27:27 THE MESSAGE.

26. See Matthew 27:33.

27. See Dr. Henrietta C. Mears, *What the Bible Is All About* (Ventura, CA: Regal, 1998), 435.

28. Isaiah 53:5–6

29. Matthew 27:45–54 THE MESSAGE

30. Luke 11:23 THE MESSAGE

31. Genesis 3:8

32. 1 John 3:2

33. See Galatians 5:16–26.

34. Romans 7:15, 18–20 ESV

35. Psalm 51:5

36. See John 8:11.

37. J. I. Packer, with Wendy Murray Zoba, *J. I. Packer Answers Questions for Today* (Wheaton, IL: Tyndale, 2001), 11.

38. See Galatians 2:20.

39. Philippians 3:10

40. Margaret Cundiff, *Travelling Light: Through St. Mark's Gospel* (London: Triangle, 1992). See also Dorothy M. Stewart, *The Westminster Collection of Christian Prayers* (Louisville: Westminster John Knox, 2002), 49.

Chapter 2: The Life Cycle of a Dangerous Choice

1. See Matthew 4:19.

2. *Encyclopædia Britannica Online*, Encyclopædia Britannica Inc., 2012. britannica .com/EBchecked/topic/168802/Domitian.

3. See Hinckley and Lee-Thorp, *The Story of Stories*, 327.

4. e.g., see Matthew 7:15–23; 1 John 2:18–27.

5. Hinckley and Lee-Thorp, *The Story of Stories*, 328.

6. Revelation 1:11

7. Revelation 1:15 NLT

8. See Revelation 1:12–16.

9. Revelation 1:17–18 THE MESSAGE

10. Dr. Larry Crabb, *66 Love Letters: A Conversation with God That Invites You into His Story* (Nashville: Thomas Nelson, 2010), 375.

11. See Matthew 7:14.

12. Revelation 2:7

13. Revelation 2:11

14. Revelation 2:17

15. Revelation 2:26–28

16. Revelation 3:5

17. Revelation 3:12

18. Revelation 3:21

19. Revelation 21:7

20. See Revelation 1:18.

21. Revelation 2:11

22. Patrick A. Means, *Men's Secret Wars* (Grand Rapids, MI: Revell, 1999), 176.

23. James 1:13–15

24. Romans 6:23

25. Ibid.

26. See 2 Corinthians 5:17.

27. e.g., see Philippians 4:8.

28. See Psalm 119:11.

29. 1 Corinthians 10:12–13 NKJV.

30. e.g., see Romans 8:5–8; Ephesians 2:3.

31. Romans 6:12–14

32. Romans 7:15

33. Elouise Renich Fraser, *Confessions of a Beginning Theologian* (Downers Grove, IL: InterVarsity, 1998), 31.

34. John Bunyan, *A Book for Boys and Girls, or Temporal Things Spiritualized* (London: Printed for and sold by R. Tookey, at his printing house in St. Christopher's Court, in Threadneedle Street, behind the Royal Exchange, 1701), 8.

Chapter 3: Everyday Enticements

1. Jeremiah 17:9
2. Proverbs 16:28 ESV
3. Proverbs 20:19 NASB
4. e.g., see Romans 1:28–32; 2 Corinthians 12:20; 2 Timothy 3:1–5.
5. See 1 Timothy 6:10.
6. Matthew 6:20–21
7. Colossians 3:2
8. Philippians 3:20
9. Matthew 6:19

10. John Owen, "On Temptation: The Nature and Power of It; the Danger of Entering into It; and the Means of Preventing That Danger" in *The Works of John Owen*, Vol. 6, ed. William H. Goold (Carlisle, PA: Banner of Truth Trust, 1967), 150. Emphasis added.

11. This "list" was compiled as church leaders reflected on Scripture and Christian experience and sought to help believers—monks in particular—learn how to deal with sin at its root. The number of seven sins dates to Gregory the Great (c. 540–604), though similar lists of eight date earlier to Cyprian (d. 258) and John Cassian (c. 360–c. 435). Everett Ferguson, *Church History: Volume One: From Christ to Pre-Reformation: The Rise and Growth of the Church in Its Cultural, Intellectual, and Political Context* (Grand Rapids, MI: Zondervan, 2005), 320; Arthur Charles O'Neil, "Sin" in *The Catholic Encyclopedia*, Vol. 14 (New York: Robert Appleton, 1912), 4–11; see at newadvent.org/cathen/14004b.htm.

12. See Genesis 2:16–17.
13. See Genesis 2:15.
14. See John 15:4.
15. See James 4:8.
16. See John 6.

17. C. S. Lewis, "The Weight of Glory" in *The Weight of Glory and Other Addresses* (New York: Macmillan, 1949), 1–2. Originally a sermon, preached on June 8, 1941.

18. 1 Corinthians 7:31
19. From *The Westminster Confession*.
20. Philippians 1:21

21. Philip E. Howard, *Temptation: What It Is, and How to Meet It* (Philadelphia: *The Sunday School Times*, 1911), 1–2.

22. Ibid., 2. Emphasis added.

23. Dietrich Bonhoeffer, *Temptation*, trans. Kathleen Downham (London: SCM, 1963), 14.

24. Hebrews 4:15 ESV

25. See Mahesh and Bonnie Chavda, *Getting to Know the Holy Spirit* (Minneapolis: Chosen, 2011), 35–36.

26. Adapted and condensed from a list compiled by Howard Culbertson, Southern Nazarene University.

27. Scot McKnight, *Why Doesn't Anybody Talk About Sin?* (07/13/11).

28. Ibid.

29. e.g., see Leviticus 11:44–45; 19:2; 20:7; Romans 1:7; 1 Corinthians 1:2; Ephesians 1:4; 5:3; 1 Thessalonians 4:7; 2 Timothy 1:9; 1 Peter 1:15–16.

30. Oswald Chambers, *My Utmost for His Highest* (New York: Dodd, Mead & Co., 1935), reading for October 6.

31. Jerry Bridges, *The Pursuit of Holiness* (Colorado Springs: NavPress, 1978), 40.

32. 2 Corinthians 7:1

33. Hebrews 12:14

34. 1 Peter 1:14–16

35. Stewart, *The Westminster Collection of Christian Prayers*, 303.

Chapter 4: Men at the Cross

1. Romans 7:15 NLT

2. This percentage goes up to two-thirds when accounting for men who admit using porn but choose not to list it as a "temptation."

3. Roy F. Baumeister, Kathleen R. Catanese, and Kathleen D. Vohs, "Is There a Gender Difference in Strength of Sex Drive? Theoretical Views, Conceptual Distinctions and a Review of Relevant Evidence" in *Personality and Social Psychology Review* 5.3 (2001): 242–273.

4. Edward O. Laumann, John H. Gagnon, Robert T. Michael, and Stuart Michaels, *The Social Organization of Sexuality: Sexual Practices in the United States* (Chicago: University of Chicago Press, 1994).

5. OnlineMBA, 2010. See the infographic at onlinemba.com/blog/stats-on-internet-pornography/. Further sourcing embedded.

6. Ibid.

7. Ibid.

8. Kimberly J. Mitchell, David Finkelhor, and Janis Wola, "The Exposure of Youth to Unwanted Sexual Material on the Internet. A National Survey of Risk, Impact, and Prevention" in *Youth & Society* 34.3 (2003): 330–358.

9. Jerry Ropelato, "Internet Pornography Statistics," 2006. internet-filter-review.toptenreviews.com/internet-pornography-statistics.html.

10. Ibid.

11. Jill C. Manning, "The Impact of Internet Pornography on Marriage and the Family: A Review of the Research" in *Sexual Addiction & Compulsivity* 13 (2006): 131–165.

12. See Jonathan Dedmon, "Is the Internet bad for your marriage? Online affairs, pornographic sites playing greater role in divorces" press release from

American Academy of Matrimonial Lawyers (2002), 14; and Jennifer P. Schneider, "Effects of Cybersex Problems on the Spouse and Family" in *Sex and the Internet: A Guidebook for Clinicians*, ed. A. Cooper (New York: Brunner-Routledge, 2002): 169–186 (180).

13. Raymond M. Bergner and Ana J. Bridges, "The Significance of Heavy Pornography Involvement for Romantic Partners: Research and Clinical Implications" in *Journal of Sex & Marital Therapy* 28 (2002): 193–206 (197).

14. Jennifer P. Schneider, "Effects of Cybersex Addiction on the Family: Results of a Survey" in *Sexual Addiction & Compulsivity* 7 (2000): 31–58.

15. Ibid.

16. Steven Stack, Ira Wasserman, and Roger Kern, "Adult Social Bonds and Use of Internet Pornography" in *Social Science Quarterly* 85 (2004): 75–88.

17. As of 09/12/12

18. Psalm 37:8 NLT

19. Proverbs 15:1 NLT

20. James 1:19–20 NLT

21. Patricia P. Chang, MD, MHS; Daniel E. Ford, MD, MPH; Lucy A. Meoni, ScM; Nae-Yuh Wang, PhD; Michael J. Klag, MD, MPH, "Anger in Young Men and Subsequent Premature Cardiovascular Disease: The Precursors Study," The JAMA Network Archives of Internal Medicine website, April 2002, (American Medical Association, © 2012), accessed 6/15/2012, http://archinte.jamanetwork.com/article.aspx?articleid=211391

22. See 1 John 4:18.

23. M. Dugas, K. Buhr, and R. Ladouceur (2003). The role of intolerance of uncertainty in the etiology and maintenance of generalized anxiety disorder. In R. Heimber, C. L. Turk, and D. S. Mennin, eds., *Generalized Anxiety Disorder: Advances in Research and Practice* (New York: Guilford).

24. Luke 1:37 NLT

25. 2 Timothy 1:7 NLT

26. Psalm 93:3–4 NLT

27. Dr. James Emery White, "Is Porn Really That Big of a Deal?" crosswalk.com/blogs/dr-james-emery-white/is-porn-really-that-big-of-a-deal-11616838.html.

28. Based on concept originally found in Robert S. McGee, *The Search for Significance* (Nashville: Word, 1998), 28–29.

29. Daniel G. Amen, *Change Your Brain, Change Your Life* (New York: Three Rivers, 1998), 59–60.

30. Malcolm Muggeridge in *The Communion of Saints: Prayers of the Famous*, ed. Horton Davies (Grand Rapids, MI: Eerdmans, 1990).

Chapter 5: Women at the Cross

1. Chinese proverb

2. See Psalm 139:14.

3. See 1 Peter 3:4.

4. See John 3:16.

5. See Zephaniah 3:17.

6. See Deuteronomy 7:6.

7. For instance, see J. J. Exline, "Anger toward God: A New Frontier in the Study of Forgiveness" in Malika Rebai Maamri, Nehama Verbin, and Everett L. Worthington Jr., eds., *A Journey Through Forgiveness* (Oxford: Inter-Disciplinary Press, 2011). [See link to eBook (ISBN: 978-1-84888-048-1) at inter-disciplinary. net/publishing/id-press/ebooks/a-journey-through-forgiveness/] Also, J. J. Exline, "Anger toward God: A brief overview of existing research" in Psychology of Religion Newsletter, 29(1): 2004, 1–8.

8. Genesis 3:6 NLT

9. Andy Rooney

10. R. Marie Griffith, "The Promised Land of Weight Loss" at religion-online. org/showarticle.asp?title=249.

11. See Matthew 6:25–26.

12. See Matthew 6:31–34.

13. See 1 Thessalonians 5:16–18; Philippians 4:10–13.

14. "Eating to the Glory of God: How Incurable God-Lovers Should Think About Eating" at gracegems.org/C/eating_to_the_glory_of_god.htm. Emphasis added.

15. Joseph Epstein, *Gossip: The Untrivial Pursuit* (Boston: Houghton Mifflin Harcourt, 2011), 3, 14.

16. dictionary.com

17. See Proverbs 16:28.

18. See 1 Timothy 5:13.

19. See Proverbs 20:19; Psalm 15:3.

20. See Leviticus 19:16; Proverbs 26:20.

21. See James 3:6.

22. Leah McClellan, "When Does Conversation Become Gossip?" peaceful planetcommunication.com/2010/05/30/when-does-a-conversation-become-gossip -two-rules-that-might-help/.

23. Michele Benner, *Gossip or Conversation? Walking the Fine Line Between the Two* at http://motown2chitown.hubpages/Gossip-or-Conversation.

24. This is a well-known saying of Dr. Charles Stanley.

25. See Romans 5:1–2.

26. See 1 Kings 19:3–5.

27. See John 7:37.

28. See Matthew 11:28.

29. See Mark 9:24.

30. See 1 Kings 18–19.

31. Ruth Haley Barton, *Sacred Rhythms* (Downers Grove, IL: IVP, 2006), 94.

32. Stewart, *The Westminster Collection of Christian Prayers,* 183.

Chapter 6: Kelly's Story: Addiction and Grace

1. Isaiah 66:13
2. See Exodus 16:4.
3. See John 10:10.
4. Mark 3:20–21, 31–35
5. The *NIV Study Bible* 10th Anniversary Edition (Grand Rapids, MI: Zondervan, 1995).
6. See "The Three C's" of Al-Anon.
7. Gerald G. May, MD, *Addiction and Grace* (San Francisco: HarperCollins, 1988), 3–4.
8. Ibid.
9. Brennan Manning with James H. Hancock, *Posers, Fakers, and Wannabees: Unmasking the Real You* (Colorado Springs: NavPress, 2003), 22–23.
10. See Ephesians 2:3 NASB.
11. See Romans 5:8.
12. Luke 23:34
13. Adapted from a list compiled by Howard Culbertson, Southern Nazarene University.
14. Stewart, *The Westminster Collection of Christian Prayers*, 104.

Chapter 7: Michael's Story: Worried to Death

1. Walter Wangerin Jr., *Letters From the Land of Cancer* (Grand Rapids, MI: Zondervan, 2010), 42.
2. Ibid., 43.
3. Frank Freed, PhD, *Breaking Free When You're Feeling Trapped* (Wheaton, IL: Harold Shaw, 1997), 46.
4. Edmund Bourne, PhD, and Laura Garano, *Coping With Anxiety* (Oakland, CA: New Harbinger, 2003), 44.
5. Proverbs 3:5
6. See Psalm 46:10.
7. See 2 Timothy 3:14–17; Hebrews 4:12–13.
8. See Bourne, *Coping With Anxiety*, 44.
9. See Genesis 37–50.
10. See Alex McFarland, *Stand: Seeking the Way of God—A Discovery of Genesis 37–47* (Carol Stream, IL: Tyndale, 2009), 34–35.
11. Psalm 46:10–11
12. Nahum 1:7
13. 1 Peter 3:18
14. John 3:16
15. John 20:21–22
16. 1 John 5:3–4

17. Wangerin, *Letters From the Land of Cancer*, 199

18. Revelation 22:1–5 THE MESSAGE

19. See Bourne, *Coping With Anxiety,* 44.

20. C. S. Lewis, "Giving All to Christ" in *Devotional Classics,* eds. Foster and Smith, 9.

21. See 1 John 4:7–16.

22. See Matthew 6:25–34.

23. See 1 John 5:1–13.

24. Stewart, *The Westminster Collection of Christian Prayers*, 278.

Chapter 8: Mark's Story: Coming Clean With a Secret War

1. "Mark" and "Ashley" are pseudonyms. Their names were changed to protect their identities. Sue Cameron, a writer and blogger in Texas, contributed to this story. Portions adapted from Sue Cameron, "Gasping for Air" in *Breakaway* (April 2008): 14–18.

2. 1 Thessalonians 4:3–5

3. See under "How Can I Overcome Temptation?" in chapter 2.

4. Patrick A. Means, *Men's Secret Wars* (Grand Rapids, MI: Revell, 1999), 176.

5. Peter Marshall, *Mr. Jones, Meet the Master* (New York: Revell, 1949).

6. Means, *Men's Secret Wars,* 177–178.

7. Ibid., 225–226.

8. Robert S. McGee, *The Search for Significance, Student Edition* (Nashville: W, 2003), 105.

9. John Wesley, *Renew My Heart* (Uhrichsville, OH: Barbour, 2011), 12–13.

10. Drawn from a similar list in Means, *Men's Secret Wars,* 27.

11. Bryce Nelson, "The Addictive Personality: Common Traits Are Found" in *The New York Times Science Section* (01/18/83).

12. Means, *Men's Secret Wars,* 27–28.

13. John 15:13

14. Created by Arnie Cole, EdD, Pamela Ovwigho, PhD, and Michael Ross at the Center for Bible Engagement. The descriptions are drawn from the goTandem Spiritual Growth Model, which is based on research with more than 100,000 people over an eight-year period. Note: We've observed yet another group of people who aren't quite captured by either the Skeptic or Seeker categories. These folks reject the Bible and Christianity, but generally don't seem concerned with spiritual matters, temptations, eternity, etc.

15. Shane Claiborne, Jonathan Wilson-Hartgrove, and Enuma Okoro, *Common Prayer: A Liturgy for Ordinary Radicals* (Grand Rapids, MI: Zondervan, 2010), 337.

Chapter 9: Danielle's Story: Am I *Struggling,* or Am I Just Plain *Defeated?*

1. 1 Corinthians 10:13

2. See Romans 8:37.

3. Judges 6:12

4. See Ecclesiastes 1:9.

5. Mark 12:30–31

6. Francis Chan, with Mark Beuving, *Living Crazy Love: An Interactive Workbook for Individual or Small-Group Study* (Colorado Springs: David C. Cook, 2011), 35.

7. Quoted in Christopher Coppernoll, *Soul 2 Soul* (Nashville: W, 1998), 47, 49.

8. Stewart, *The Westminster Collection of Christian Prayers*, 225.

Chapter 10: Unmasking the REAL Me

1. Acts 2:44–47

2. David Wilkerson, *Victory Over Sin and Self* (Grand Rapids, MI: Revell, 1994), 23.

3. Galatians 6:2

4. Amy Mandelker and Elizabeth Powers, *Pilgrim Souls* (New York: Simon & Schuster, 1999), 120.

5. Wilkerson, *Victory Over Sin and Self,* 23.

6. Janet Lees, "God of Good Ideas," © Janet Lees, from *Seeing Christ in Others*, ed. Geoffrey Duncan (Atlanta: Canterbury, 1998).

Ending Point: Giving Grace Another Chance

1. See Matthew 20:1–16.

2. Matthew 20:13–15

3. Jonah 4:9

4. See Jonah 4:1–11.

5. Matthew 5:21–22

Appendix: Calvin, Luther, and Arminius

1. See 1 John 3:3.

2. See 1 John 3:5–10.

3. C. S. Lewis, *God in the Dock: Essays on Theology and Ethics* (Grand Rapids, MI: Eerdmans, 1970), 128.

4. C. S. Lewis, *Mere Christianity* (New York: HarperCollins, 1952), 154.

5. Acquired by Michael Ross during an email dialogue (06/19/12).

6. See John Calvin, *Institutes of the Christian Religion* (Peabody, MA: Hendrickson, 2007, rev. ed.).

7. C. P. Krauth, "The Conservative Reformation and Its Theology: As Represented in the Augsburg Confession, and in the History and Literature of the Evangelical Lutheran Church," *Part IX: The Specific Doctrines of the Conservative Reformation: Original Sin* (Philadelphia: J. B. Lippincott, 1875), 335–455.

8. Philippians 2:13

9. *Manual/2009–2013 Church of the Nazarene,* "Articles of Faith: No. 7 Prevenient Grace," (Kansas City, MO: Nazarene, 2009), 31.

10. See Canons of Dort, Article 8. View at forms.reformed.org.ua/Dordt%20 Canons/all/.

11. Compare various Calvinistic viewpoints. See *SBC Life: Journal of the Southern Baptist Convention,* "The TULIP of Calvinism," by Malcolm B. Yarnell III, PhD, at sbclife.org/Articles/2006/04/sla8.asp (contrast with articles posted at reformed.org/calvinism/index.html [Center for Reformed Theology and Apologetics]).

12. *Brief Statement: Doctrinal Position of the Missouri Synod,* "Of Conversion: No. 13" (St. Louis: CPH, 1932), 4.

13. Consider Roger E. Olson, *Arminian Theology: Myths and Realities* (Downers Grove, IL: IVP Academic, 2006).

14. John Calvin, *Commentary on John,* "John 6:41–45" (Grand Rapids, MI: Christian Classics Ethereal Library), 150.

15. See James White, *The Sovereign Grace of God: A Biblical Study of the Doctrines of Calvinism* (Lindenhurst, NY: Reformation, 2003). Also articles and discussions at monergism.com (Christian Publication Resource Foundation).

16. *The Book of Concord: The Confessions of the Lutheran Church,* "The Solid Declaration of the Formula of Concord: Art. II, Free Will, or Human Powers," par. 59, bookofconcord.org/sd-freewill.php (accessed 09/25/12).

17. *Brief Statement: Doctrinal Position of the Missouri Synod,* "Of Conversion: No. 14," 4.

18. See "The Use of the Means of Grace: A Statement on the Practice of Word and Sacrament" at elca.org/Growing-In-Faith/Worship/Learning-Center/ The-Use-of-the-Means-of-Grace.aspx.

19. See various articles and discussions at evangelicalarminians.org/?q=index (Society of Evangelical Arminians).

20. Southern Baptist Convention, "Southern Baptist Faith and Message, No. 5: God's Purpose of Grace" (1999–2012), sbc.org/bfm/bfm2000.asp#iv (accessed 10/01/12). Also see R. C. Sproul, *Chosen by God: Knowing God's Perfect Plan for His Glory and His Children* (Carol Stream, IL: Tyndale, 1994).

21. *The Book of Concord: The Confessions of the Lutheran Church,* "The Smalcald Articles: Part III, Art. III, Of the False Repentance of the Papists," par. 43, bookofconcord.org/smalcald.php (accessed 10/02/12).

22. John 10:27–28

23. *Manual/2009–2013 Church of the Nazarene,* 31.

A Proven Path to a Thriving Walk With Christ